Signs and wonders today

SIGNS AND WONDERS TODAY

Donald Bridge

INTER-VARSITY PRESS

Inter-Varsity Press
38 De Montfort Street, Leicester LE1 7GP, England

First published 1985
Reprinted 1985

British Library Cataloguing in Publication Data
Bridge, Donald
    Signs and wonders today.
    1. Gifts, Spiritual
    I. Title
    234'.12   BT767

ISBN 0–85110–467–3

Set in Bembo

Typeset in Great Britain by TJB Photosetting Ltd. South
Witham, Lincolnshire.

Printed and bound in Great Britain by
Cox & Wyman Ltd, Reading

*Inter-Varsity Press is the publishing division of the
Universities and Colleges Christian Fellowship (formerly the
Inter-Varsity Fellowship), a student movement linking
Christian Unions in universities and colleges throughout the
United Kingdom and the Republic of Ireland, and a member
movement of the International Fellowship of Evangelical
Students. For information about local and national activities
write to UCCF, 38 De Montfort Street, Leicester LE1 7GP.*

Contents

Acknowledgments

As so often before, I owe a debt to the patience, sympathy and skill of Beryl Belcher who somehow turns my long-hand into a neat manuscript. John Freeman and Pauline Stock gave badly needed help with paragraph titles when I was far from home and publishers. To my friends, I say thank you.

Donald Bridge

1

A reason for writing

One cold January week a few years ago, I was guest-speaker at a conference in the English Midlands for Malaysian students, doctors, nurses and teachers. It was a fascinating and humbling experience. Here were fine young people, most of whom had encountered Christ and submitted to him in the last few years or even months. We studied the Bible together as I led them through Paul's second letter to Timothy under the general theme of 'The making of a Christian leader'. (Almost by definition, most of those present were potential leaders for the churches to which they would return in Asia.) There was a great deal of warm response. Many of them spoke kindly and appreciatively of my knowledge and understanding (they felt) of the Chinese mind and the Malaysian culture. This surprised me, because my ignorance of those subjects is profound and regrettable. What was actually happening (as I realized before long) was the common experience of the regular Bible expositor – the Scripture was speaking for itself and the Holy Spirit was applying the truth, with a relevance that does not spring from mere topicality but is inherent in *divine and eternal truth*.

The comments and discussions began to show me one problem looming large in many minds. Malaysia (I dimly grasped) is divided between rather sophisticated Chinese in the west and a literally Stone-Age populace in the east.

In the educated west, churches are organized well, contain third-generation Christians, feature a great desire for knowledge and training, and reflect a slightly cold and academic Chinese mentality. In the primitive east where witchcraft, spiritism and animism prevail (though under Muslim pressures) first-generation converts are making astonished discoveries of the first elements of the gospel, are responding with the unrestrained emotions which come naturally to them, and find themselves in confrontation with wonder-working priests and witch-doctors of the old religion. They are moving into a near-revival situation spilling over from Indonesia where marvellous reports for years have spoken of healings, exorcisms, remarkable deliverance, dreams, visions, miracles, and phenomenal growth.

The result was very real tension. Some of the Chinese students were frankly embarrassed by their naive eastern counterparts. Some of them felt reluctantly drawn to mission work in the east but were repelled or troubled by what they expected to find. Some were worshipping in 'charismatic' churches here in Britain where the same interest in 'wonders' was focused and yet somehow it came out differently. *There* it seemed to be 'see what God is doing'. *Here* it was more like, 'listen to what you should do to prove you are Spirit-filled'. Was that really the same? British missionaries present showed similar tensions. Some were home from the Stone-Age tribes and were wildly enthusiastic. They wanted to work up the same kind of thing here (that may be unfair, but it is how this observer, though predisposed to sympathize, felt about it). I was slightly embarrassed. Other missionaries were not half so sure. They spoke of excesses, of indiscipline, of foolish division, of barely-Christianized superstition, of the desperate need for sound and sane Bible-teaching. In the same breath they acknowledged a life and vitality, an expectancy and immediacy, a childlike trust in the promises of God often sadly lacking on the 'home front'.

I had a very busy time. Some of the conversations humbled me; I had more need to receive than to give. Others disturbed me. There was a tendency to make excitement a rival to sober thinking; dreams and visions a preference to Bible searching, and experience an enemy of theology. That was true only of some, but I noticed it and winced.

The supernatural and the miraculous

What had happened was this. In a particularly colourful and concentrated manner, and among some of the most delightful and courteous Christians, I had come across once again an issue that is rarely absent when followers of Jesus get together in the 1980s. It is the whole issue of the supernatural and the miraculous.

The Christian who takes his Bible seriously finds himself fighting a battle on no less than three fronts when he approaches the miraculous. On one hand he is confronted by a mechanistic view of science which sees the universe as a closed system in which everything is locked in a series of cause-and-effect. Everything is predictable. Everything follows unalterable 'laws'. Partly because of the sweeping and unproven assertions of some atheistic scientists, and partly because of a genuine confusion of thought, many intelligent people simply take it for granted that science has disproved and dismissed any possibility of the miraculous, of the supernatural, or indeed of *God* (in any dynamic sense of that word). The argument (if it is ever put clearly in words, for it is often no more than a general feeling) goes something like this. 'The universe is governed by laws. Either that means there is no need for a "god" since the laws are self-explanatory – or possibly it means that "god" is the framer of those laws and therefore cannot keep interfering with them and breaking them. In either case, the God of the Bible seems to be ruled out.'

9

This is all based on so many false assumptions and false conclusions that we shall have to return to it later and answer it. Sufficient to say that the Christian is up against it in a most persuasive form. The assertion that God answers prayer, or God intervenes, or God does and did what the Bible describes, is met with the kind of pitying incredulity usually reserved for people who claim that the world is flat or that a copper bracelet cures arthritis or that fairies live at the bottom of their garden.

There is another front to fight on, too. Ironically, at a time when mankind is supposed to have grown up and become totally secular, there is enormous interest in and appetite for the irrational, the occult, the spectacular, and contrary-to-nature. More people read horoscopes than read the Bible. There are more practising witches in England than there are Baptist ministers. Station bookstores are festooned with best-sellers which assure us with straight faces that the Pyramids affect our fate, that space-aliens built air-strips in Iron-Age Peru, that your marriage could founder on the fact that you were born under the wrong planet, that your mental capacity can be increased by wrapping your legs around your neck and chanting the names of Hindu spirits. The more bizarre, it seems, the more believable. Now the Christian stands firmly against all this. Some of it is dangerous and the rest is nonsense. The Christian gospel is mind-enlarging and mind-renewing; it has no stake in superstition and credulity. G.K. Chesterton loved to point out in his Father Brown detective stories that it is precisely the mind closed to God that is thereby open to the most ridiculous falsehoods and superstitions. 'People readily swallow the untested claims of this, that and the other. It's drowning all your old rationalism and scepticism, it's coming in like a sea; and the name of it is superstition. It's the first effect of not believing in God that you lose your common sense and can't see things as they are.'

But of course if the Christian stands against bizarre nonsense and occult dabbling, he is accused of being inconsistent. 'You object to reading the stars but you believe in wise men who followed one. You object to superstition but you believe that praying in an empty room in America makes something happen in China. You object to magic but you favour miracles. What's the difference?' So the argument goes. Again, it is an argument filled with holes, but it has to be faced.

And that leads to a third line of battle. Perhaps partly as a human riposte to all this, perhaps partly as a divine reply to it, the Christian church finds itself in the final quarter of the twentieth century having to come to terms with a flood of 'signs and wonders' within its own ranks.

Books with accounts of miracles, healings, dramatic deliverances and colourful experiences weigh down the religious bookshelves. Publishers agree that evangelical experience and charismatic excitement sell well. Few Christian students are unaware of some popular and successful church nearby which draws large numbers and claims exciting phenomena. As a matter of plain statistics, the presently fastest-growing wings of the church feature a heady mixture of warm affection, eventful celebration and the exercise of 'spiritual gifts' and miraculous activities. The new churches of Africa, Asia and South America are growing phenomenally and very many of them have the expectation of the extraordinary in the everyday (if that is not a contradiction in terms!). At least some of these home-churches and third-world movements have leaders whose love for Scripture, faithful preaching of the gospel and consistent godly living are matters for the most profound gratitude. Moreover they make constant reference to the Bible in support of their style of church life.

Naivety and muddled thinking

Yet there are problems. Some Christians affected by the enthusiasm and blessing become irrational and unteachable. An unhealthy obsession with the exciting (and the positively zany) marks their Christian life. Discipline is dismissed as legalism, organization is condemned as relying on the flesh, emotion becomes the measure of spirituality. Sensible leadership is dismissed in favour of transparently manufactured 'prophecy'. Reading the Bible only 'when you feel like it' is regarded as superior to the regular cultivation of the Quiet Time. Alleged evidences of the activity of God are offered which make the objective observer blush with embarrassment. It is no glory to God to attribute to the fount of all wisdom crudities of naivety and muddled thinking. An indisputably sincere Christian told me not long ago of a remarkable 'healing'. His wife fell downstairs and broke her leg. 'I could tell it was broken', this layman assured me cheerfully. He laid hands on it for healing but it still hurt. Then he realized what had happened. The pain was not the broken leg but a 'spirit of pain' (sic) which had entered his wife when she opened her mouth to cry in fear and shock as she fell! Now all was simple. The spirit was duly cast out, the pain disappeared, and the break was healed. Apart from the use of prayer there was simply nothing scriptural or Christian in this whole anecdote. Pseudo-medical nonsense was allied to some kind of spirit-animism and the package presented as a triumph of the gospel.

That kind of super-spirituality can seem very attractive and impressive. Its mixture of hearty commitment and cheerful expectancy could teach some more cautious Christians a thing or two. But it is riddled with dubious presuppositions and sits loosely to real Bible teaching that any long-term impact is going to be very limited. It puts the whole centre-of-gravity of Christian living in a place where historic biblical Christianity has never put it.

The modern Christian, then, finds himself in a situation not unlike the one of the rather more exotic wrestling-matches seen on Saturday-afternoon television. He is constantly struggling with two different opponents at once, the materialist and the magician. At the same time he has a well-meaning but erratic colleague who gets in his way, trips him up, and generally causes as many problems to him as to his opponents.

There is more than one warning in the Bible about keeping our feet firm and not wasting our blows in the spiritual conflict. (1 Corinthians 9:26; Ephesians 6:11ff.) It is my hope that this examination of the miraculous in the Bible will help some readers to 'wrestle' and to 'stand' with some prospect of success. That will require the patience to look carefully at a whole wide area of Bible teaching. It is perhaps less exciting than mixing a few favourite proof-texts with some dramatic anecdotes, but in the long run it will be more fruitful.

2

A study in confrontation

Towards the end of the Bronze Age in the Middle East, a semitic people stormed into the land of Canaan and conquered it. The ashes of the cities they burned can be fingered today. The abrupt change of culture which their arrival caused can be evidenced by archaeologists. More importantly, the story they brought with them has influenced the world ever since. There are more people today than populated the whole world at that time who would claim to establish their way of life on that story. For the invading Israelites spoke of a leader Moses, now dead, who had led them out of slavery in Egypt. They spoke of their God *Yahweh*, the *Lord*, the Eternal One, who had been the real power behind the rescue. He had delivered them, made a covenant with them, and given them his Law.

The coming of that energetic people, their conquest of a land which often claims the world headlines to this day, and the fact that they carried such a faith with them, is not a fable or a fancy but a verifiable historical fact. The book of Exodus claims to give the divine explanation and interpretation of that undoubted fact. In doing so it presents most of the truths, concepts, images and doctrines on which the rest of the Bible is built. 'Exodus' is the seed-bed of Scripture, from which almost all else grows.

Here is *God* – known by his personal name and nature; righteous, merciful, active, almighty (Exodus 3:6–15).

Here are *the people of God* – a family that becomes a nation; a nation through whom God's world-purposes will emerge; Israel which becomes the international Church of God (Exodus 19:5–6; 1 Peter 2:9).

Here is *redemption* – the basic fact forever scored on Israel's memory, that God saw them, loved them, chose them, saved them. Much later the same word 'redemption' speaks of the new demonstration of power and love by which God, acting in Jesus Christ rescues a people from the bondage of Satan and presents them to God (Ephesians 2:11–13; 1 Peter 1:18–19).

Here is *Passover* – the annual memorial of God's saving work, a chain of festivals linking every generation, but finding total fulfilment and meaning in Christ our Passover Lamb (*see* 1 Corinthians 5:6–8) and in the church's central sacrament of the Lord's Supper (Luke 22:7–19).

Here is *Law* – the totally new concept of absolute unchangeable standards expressing the direct will of the righteous God, and written down in a visible code. Without it (in at least some diluted form) social and civilized life is impossible. With it, the reader is driven to an awareness of his failure, weakness and guilt, and thence to a sight of the pardon and new life that is to be found in Christ alone (Galatians 3:23ff.).

Here, finally, is the whole Bible concept of God who is *known by what he does*. What he did at this particular time re-echoes through laws and psalms, prophecies and promises.

Remember the wonderful works that he has done,
his miracles and the judgments he uttered.

He sent Moses his servant,
and Aaron whom he had chosen.
They wrought his signs among them,
and miracles in the land of Ham (Psalm 105:5, 26–27).

A thousand years later an apostle writes to Greek converts from a pagan and licentious society,

> Now these things happened to *them*...they were written down for *our* instruction (1 Corinthians 10:11). (My italics)

Notice two things in these quotations. The facts are regarded as strictly historical...'These things happened...' and the language of miracle is used...'wonderful work, miracles, judgments....signs and miracles'. God was at work. He acted freely, not confined by things as they are, nor limited by what normally happens. He did what man cannot do, in ways man cannot understand or imitate. Here, at the very beginning of the story of God's salvation, we have the supernatural, the special, the extraordinary. Explain it in terms of politics and economics, of migrations and battles, and you are saying something quite different. The story can be fitted into history but cannot be explained in terms of mere human activity. We can date it with some certainty, but it is touched with eternity. We can identify some of the men involved, but God was at work. The nineteenth dynasty commenced in Egypt in 1319 BC. Its first king, Seti I, was probably the 'new king over Egypt, who did not know Joseph' (Exodus 1:8). His successor, Rameses II, is almost certainly the Pharaoh confronted by Moses (Exodus 2:23ff.). He was an obsessive builder who reconstructed the cities of Pithom and Ra'amses with semitic slave-labour (Exodus 1:11) housed in Goshen, east of the Nile delta (Genesis 47:27). Some of the journey of the freed slaves through Sinai can be reconstructed, and their arrival in Canaan with sword and fire can be traced with ease by modern archaeology.

History, then. But more than human history. It has often been commented that history is his-story. The Bible makes it clear that God intervened. Hence a 'mighty hand

and an outstretched arm' (Deuteronomy 26:8). Hence the plagues on Egypt, the crossing of the Red Sea, the amazing preservation of the life of thousands in an almost waterless and foodless desert. Hence the inescapable and unavoidable 'miracles'. But here is a bonus, too. For the whole subject of 'signs and wonders' crops up here in a particularly vivid way. Here is a detailed account of the miraculous. Here are vital principles established which are fundamental to answering some of the questions we have posed from today's world. Here, quite certainly, is the beginning of an answer to the question, how can God break his own laws? Here are some facts that will surprise some enthusiastic miracle-seeking Christians. Here is the miraculous in perspective; God's perspective and therefore the true one.

The story is told of an American congregation which included some negroes accustomed to answering the preacher as he went along. On one occasion they were addressed by someone with 'liberal' leanings, tending to dismiss the miracles of the Bible. He referred in his sermon to the Israelites crossing the Red Sea.

'Praise de Lord', shouted a negro. 'Takin' all dem children through de deep waters. What a mighty miracle!'

The preacher frowned. 'It was not a miracle', he explained condescendingly. 'They were doubtless in marsh-land, the tide was ebbing, and the children of Israel picked their way across in six inches of water.'

'Praise de Lord!', shouted the negro unabashed. 'Drownin' all dem Egyptians in six inches of water. What a mighty miracle!'

The tale is salutary (if possibly apocryphal). The events of the Exodus are an account of the mighty action of a sovereign God. In detail they contain very many natural phenomena; the Bible almost goes out of its way to say so. But the sum of it all was a powerful act of God. By God's intervention, at God's appointed time, and by God's outstretched arm, a world dictator was confronted, a powerful false religion was humiliated, thousands of people were rescued from a hopeless situation, and a rabble of slaves was transformed into the beginnings of a nation for God.

The plagues of Egypt – their purpose

There is enormous significance in this story, related in chapters 5 to 10 of Exodus. This is very much more than a splendid Sunday School lesson to be stretched out gratifyingly over six Sundays, or a spectacular Hollywood film with great scope for special effects. First of all, the plagues are prefaced by *a revelation of God*. Constantly in chapter 6 God announces 'I will…I will' (verses 1–8). He speaks both as *El Shaddai*, the Almighty, and *Yahweh*, the Eternal.

In soaring promises God says 'I will bring you out', 'I will deliver you', 'I will redeem you', 'I will take you for my people', 'I will be your God'. These great promises express the deeply religious and spiritual purpose of what God is doing; they are to be his people, he is to be their God, and the promises finish where they began – I am the Lord. The whole magnificent message is sealed at both ends with the authority of the living and faithful God. It is this that sets the 'plagues of Egypt' in their right perspective.

Secondly, *judgment is announced*. If the facts are the plagues, what is the strategy? What we see now described is a succession of repetitive stories in which water is turned to blood, swarms of frogs overrun the land, a disease sweeps through the capital, and all reaching a mounting climax with the destruction of Egyptian family life. *But what is it all for?* It was not only a revelation of God, but it was an announcement of judgment. This note is seen immediately. 'Now you shall see what I will do to Pharaoh' (Exodus 6:1). 'I will redeem you with an outstretched arm and with great acts of judgment,' (Exodus 6:6). The word 'redeem' here (*go-el*) is a word from the law courts. It implies the claiming of rights in lands and family; a judgment in favour of one party and therefore against another. A divine court has been set up; Pharaoh is in the wrong, God is in the right. Pharaoh is driven to admit this at one point under the hammer-blows of successive plagues. 'I have sinned this time; the LORD is in the right, and I and my people are in the wrong' (Exodus 9:27).

But the judgment is against not only a hard-hearted tyrant and an unjust society. There is *war declared in the realm of the supernatural*. Egypt was riddled with religion, priestcraft and superstition. It was dominated by priest-magicians who had apparently impressive powers. The New Testament refers to two of them by name. Now almost every feature in Egypt's life, and very many of these detailed features involving the plagues, have a strongly religious significance: the river Nile was regarded as divine. Pharaoh was in some sense a god incarnate. The clash of the two systems is seen just under the surface of many of the confrontations. 'Who is the LORD that I should heed his voice…?' asks Pharaoh contemptuously (Exodus 5:2). 'I will redeem you with an outstretched arm and with great acts of judgment, and I will take you for my people, and I will be your God;' (Exodus 6:6) announces the Lord. And specifically when threatening the onset of the plagues God says '…the Egyptians shall know that I am the LORD, when I stretch forth my hand upon Egypt…' (Exodus 7:5). Most clearly of all, at the time of the Passover and the smiting of the first-born of Egypt, God says, 'I will pass through the land of Egypt that night… and on all the gods of Egypt I will execute judgments'. Nothing could be more clear than that. And this is precisely what God does in great detail. There is a startling link between several of the plagues and several of the Egyptian deities and it may well be that if we knew more of Egyptian life, we would see an almost total interrelationship between the blows that were struck and certain details of Egyptian religion.

In the first plague the Nile was turned to blood (Exodus 7:17–21). The river Nile was sacred and regarded as a deity. It was the god who by the annual flooding provided water and soil, essential for the life of the nation. It was the god to whom Israel's babies were offered when their slave conditions were at their worst.

A second disaster brought swarms of frogs. These creatures were associated with the god Hapi and the goddess Heqt who gave increase of family and assisted at childbirth. Sacred indeed – but thousands of them crawling in the food and the bedding made sacredness a mockery (Exodus 8:1–7).

A fourth plague brought immense numbers of flying insects (Exodus 8:20–21): very likely beetles. We all know of the scarab, the sacred beetle which was the emblem of fertility. In these swarms there was fertility with a vengeance! The fifth stroke was a disease which attacked domestic animals (Exodus 9:1–3). In Egyptian religion the ram, the goat and the bull were all sacred. Next came an epidemic of boils and scabs (Exodus 9:8–12). Personal cleanliness was actually part of religious devotion to the Egyptian, which was the reason why they removed all of their body hairs. The ninth blow brought darkness over all the earth; in effect the sun-god Rah was seen to be eclipsed (Exodus 10:21–23). The tenth plague brought the killing of the first-born (Exodus 11:4–6) and it must be remembered that the first-born of Pharaoh was the next incarnation of one of their gods, and that the first-born of every Egyptian family ensured the continuation of the sacred Egyptian master-race. So the whole succession of calamities is seen as a succession of 'blows' or 'strokes' (the word 'plague' can mean either) which are executed against the gods of Egypt.

But the confrontation between Moses and Pharaoh also illustrates another very important feature – *God's direction of nature*. Although repeatedly the cataclysms that fall upon

Egypt are attributed to the hand of God, there is a constant emphasis on the fact that the means which God employs are what we would nowadays call the laws of nature. The actual instruments do not strike us as the slightest bit supernatural. The waters of Egypt, vast numbers of frogs, gnats, beetles, cattle disease, scabs and boils, heavy hail storms, attacks of locusts and darkness over the land; all of these in themselves are natural enough phenomena. There is even a fairly natural and logical progression from one disaster to another.

If we assume that the Nile turning to blood is to be understood in terms of other Bible references, we have here a language of appearance rather than biology. The water turned red and offensive. Moses first challenged Pharaoh at what was presumably the spring religious ceremony when the hoped-for flood of the Nile, carrying water and silt down from far-away Ethiopia, would make the continuation of agricultural life possible in Egypt. To persuade the divine Nile to oblige as usual, religious ceremonies were held beside its waters. The melting of snow and heavy rains up-river brought floods at some unpredictable time between June and October; obviously the sooner the better. Sometimes two things went wrong: immense quantities of red mud from Abyssinia (*i.e.* from the Red Nile rather than the White Nile) discoloured the whole of the water as it reached Egypt. Occasionally too, tiny bacteria and plankton poisoned the water, giving it a red appearance, an offensive smell and a bitter taste. Is this what happened as Moses smote the water? We are certainly told that some Egyptians were able to avoid the worst effects by filtering the Nile water through the nearby sand and making it possible to drink after all (Exodus 7:24).

From this the swarming of frogs would follow naturally as they leave the poisoned water; in fact they often left fresh water at this time of the year in great numbers. In turn the swarms of insects whether they were gnats, beetles or mosquitoes, would again follow logically. The poisoned water drives the frogs inland and they die; the insects swarm in the rotting bodies of the frogs. Alternatively, the fields are flooded as autumn has now come, and the shallow water breeds the mosquitoes.

In the fourth plague we find Pharaoh worshipping once more at the riverside; this presumably for the ceremony at the end of the flooding season, now well into the autumn ('...wait for Pharaoh, as he goes out to the water', Exodus 8:20). If the earlier insects were a direct result of the carcasses of the frogs rotting, these flies could be the hatching of eggs that were laid in the carcasses at that earlier period. The Greek Old Testament written in Egypt uses the phrase 'dog flies' which had a very powerful sting. In turn the domestic animals are infected by a disease quite possibly spread by the insects; this could well be the dreaded anthrax. Again there is a logical progression in an irritating and defiling skin disease, also quite possibly spread by insects, or perhaps the still well-known Nile scab which precisely follows the ebbing of the flood. Deuteronomy 28:27 suggests that boils, ulcers, scurvy and itch were common problems in Egypt.

The pressure increases
The disasters now hurry on to a climax, though there is certainly nothing miraculous in itself about heavy hailstorms and the locusts which follow. Locusts are in every generation one of the most dreaded scourges of Egypt. They obviously do not arise directly from the earlier disasters, but their arrival fits the time schedule if we now assume that we are approaching the end of the winter and moving towards spring when we know that the Passover was celebrated. It is noticeable that the locusts are brought into the area by the natural phenomenom of an east wind, which is what in fact normally does bring them from their breeding grounds in the Arabian steppes. Equally natur-

ally, a west wind blew them into the Red Sea and ended the plague. The penultimate disaster is 'a darkness that could be felt' (Exodus 10:21). A particular wind to this day in Egypt, called the 'hamsin', often blows for fifty days into the springtime, ending shortly before Passover and bringing sandstorms from the desert. A hamsin in the 1970s left Jericho with visibility nil.

So throughout the dramatic story the God of the supernatural is seen directly at work, striking one blow after another against his spiritual enemies, but employing as his instruments the natural world and its laws which are part of his own creation. A Jewish Christian writer of unimpeachable orthodoxy suggests 'apart from the last there is nothing supernatural in the plagues. They are intensifications of natural troubles which have plagued Egypt down through the centuries. Like most biblical miracles they point to God's *control of nature* rather than the power to do that which is contrary to nature.'[1]

Nevertheless, this is God directly at work. We have seen that he was active in revelation, in judgment and in holy warfare, so each plague comes precisely when God commands it. Each is preceded by a face-to-face confrontation between God's servant and the representative of Egyptian religion. Moses usually prefaces a plague with a symbolic action, and almost invariably the disaster comes to an end when Moses commands it to; usually because Pharaoh has either admitted hurt, pleaded for cessation or made some compromise offer.

'Be it as you say', cries Moses at the end of one such disaster, 'that you may know that there is no one like the Lord your God, The frogs shall depart...' (Exodus 8:10). Hence there is used the remarkable phrase 'This is the finger of God' (Exodus 8:19): the very expression that is used of the miracles of Jesus (Luke 11:20). From beginning to end the initiative is with God. The power comes from God. 'Whether God brings about this event by what we call

23

natural causes or not is quite immaterial.'[2] There is one other feature which heavily underlines the direct activity of God. That is the remarkable separation which God creates between the people of Israel in the land of Goshen and the Egyptian people in the rest of the empire. 'Thus I will put a division between your people and my people' (Exodus 8:23) announces the Lord as he brings swarms of flies upon the Egyptians but preserves the Israelites from their worst effects. And even more clearly '...that you may know that the Lord makes a distinction between the Egyptians and Israel' (Exodus 11:7. Notice that here, judgment on the one hand and redemption on the other are in mind). This is a vital spiritual principle which God is underlining by his direct activity; the separation, the distinctiveness of the people of God.

Final confrontation
Hard on the heels of the natural disasters came the terrible blow of the smiting of the first-born (Exodus 12:29-30). Here we seem to be in a different dimension. No normal disease (bubonic plague and poliomyelitis have been suggested) can be made to fit the death of only the eldest son in each Egyptian family, the preservation of every Israelite who sheltered under the Passover blood, and the focusing of the whole grim episode into the span of one dark night.

This in turn is followed by one of the most spectacular events in the whole Bible, and one which finds echoes throughout the rest of Scripture. The fleeing slaves found themselves trapped between the sea, the steppe-land and the pursuing Egyptians. God intervened and they escaped with 'the waters being a wall to them on their right hand and on their left' (Exodus 14:22). The enemy tried to pursue them and were drowned. It was an adventure celebrated forever as a mighty act of God, a supreme example of salvation. 'Fear not, stand firm, and see the salvation of the

24

Lord', was Moses' magnificent invitation and summary (Exodus 14:13).

Yet even here the cross-links between God's intervention and the usual 'laws of nature' are clearly seen. They have been obscured to some extent by children's illustrated Bibles and Hollywood film epics. The dramatic picture of the 'walls of water' is precisely that; a dramatic picture. A book as impeccably conservative as the IVP *Tyndale Commentary* explains, 'If these were reedy salt marshes, with a soft bottom,...then a culmination of ebb-tide and strong wind could dry them temporarily, long enough for a light-armed group to scamper across.' The metaphor of the waters being a wall 'is no more to be taken literally than when Ezra 9:8 says that God has given him a "wall" ... It is a poetic metaphor to explain why the Egyptian chariots could not sweep in to right and left, and cut Israel off.'[3]

So the natural forces at work are described in some detail; 'a strong east wind all night'... 'the waters were divided'... the Egyptian chariot wheels 'clogging...so that they drove heavily'... and with grim and terrible inevitability, the waters 'returned'. Yet throughout these natural events (that is, the use of natural agencies) the divine power and initiative is equally emphasized. God presences himself protectively between fugitives and pursuers, 'the LORD drove the sea back', 'the LORD...looked down... and discomforted the host of the Egyptians', and 'the LORD routed the Egyptians in the midst of the sea'.

The remarkable synthesis of divine action and natural function is splendidly (if poetically) summed up in the triumphant song of Moses,

At the blast of thy nostrils the waters piled up...
Thou didst blow with thy wind, the sea covered them;...
Thou didst stretch out thy right hand,
    the earth swallowed them.   (Exodus 15:8,10,12)

It may not have been quite the Cecil B. de Mille picture, but it was dramatic and terrifying enough in all conscience. The wild night march, the roar of the rising wind, the silent beckoning path between the surging waters, the full moon of Passover sometimes shrouded by the wildly scudding clouds, the angry hiss of the returning waters and the contrasting cries of Egyptian despair and Israelite triumph;…'Thus the LORD saved Israel ' (Exodus 14:30).

More drama follows. The march into the desert of Sinai was ever remembered as the stage on which a protecting and providing God played out his wise and gracious purposes. The apostle Paul points to the wilderness adventures as carrying a special warning and example to the Christians (1 Corinthians 10:1–6). Yet wonderful though the experience was, it featured few outright miracles. Sinai is not the Sahara Desert. It is not totally incapable of supporting life, nor is it waterless and trackless. Israel took the well-marked 'Road of the Mineworkers' down the eastern coast of the western arm of the Red Sea. The route passed many water-holes, and less-frequent oases can be traced with some certainty today. A three-day journey at the likely speed of fifteen miles daily leads to Ain Hawarah with its bitter and just-usable water (presumably the Marah of Exodus 15:23). Wood from the barberry bush, if immersed in the water, exudes an aromatic sap which makes the water more palatable (verse 25). An easy day's march south reaches the splendid oasis of Wadi Gharandel, presumably the Elim of verse 27, with its many terebinth-palms still answering the biblical description and suggesting the biblical name. The little bullet-headed birds called quails still migrate in vast numbers across Sinai in the March–April period which the Bible account demands, and can be caught in their exhaustion (Exodus 16:13). The manna is another question (Exodus 16:14–31). Most of us have read descriptions of the Arabic 'man' still collected and eaten by Bedouin. It is produced by some interaction between two insects and the tamarisk twigs on which they alight. It very roughly corresponds to the scriptural description (fine, white, seed-like and sweet-tasting), and it appears after the spring rains and thus fits the time-schedule after Passover.

But that explanation is hardly adequate. The amounts of 'man' would never be enough to feed the numbers involved, it does not appear all the year round as the story requires, and it certainly does not obligingly integrate with a Sabbath-observation. The phenomenon still to be seen today provides no more than an interesting but much less impressive parallel. We must leave the last word with God, who tells us, '…and fed you with manna, which you did not know,…that he might make you know that man does not live by bread alone, but that man lives by everything that proceeds out of the mouth of the LORD' (Deuteronomy 8:3 and quoted by Jesus in Matthew 4:1–4).

The total picture

What then does this great saga tell us? At every turn in these decisive events, God is seen to be at work. He takes the initiative. His purposes are the key to the events. His salvation is the theme. Here is no mere succession of coincidences and natural opportunities grasped by rebellious slaves. Moses was not a shrewd mob leader who took masterly advantage of a succession of climatic disasters. Nor can we explain the Red Sea event in terms of an ebb-tide, a strong wind, the arrival of a meteorite, the close passage of a comet, the eruption of a volcano (to name but a few suggestions made from time to time). The timing was God's, just as the purpose was God's.

The choice of instruments was God's too. Yet as a matter of fact, the choice was curiously 'natural'. The Nile inundation, the dust-laden hamsin, the cattle murrain, the locusts from Arabia, the strong wind in the night, the turning of the tides, the helplessness of chariot wheels in deep mud, the age-old track of the mine-workers, the water-hole and the oasis; *these* were God's instruments. For the God of the supernatural is *that*, precisely because he is the God of nature. *He controls what he created.*

He created all things. The first words of the Bible picture it. Light springs into being at his command. The mountains rise from the oceans at his behest. He speaks, and the land is populated. He is independent of nature, but nature is dependent on him. Having created the world, he sustains it.

The cycle of the stars follows his command. The grass continues to grow at his behest. Summer and winter, seed-time and harvest come and go in fulfilment of his promise (*see* Genesis 8:22). All living things draw their sustenance from him. Our breath is in his hands. The very power that binds the universe together in the molecules, and the planets together in the solar system, is his. Nature is precisely nature (the word means 'as-it-is') because God is God.

What that implies, we must now explore further.

Notes for chapter two

[1]H.L. Ellison, *Exodus Daily Study Bible* (St Andrew Press, 1982), pp.40-41.
[2]H.L. Ellison in the *Daily Study Bible* and Alan Cole in the *Tyndale Commentary* both make the same point.
[3]Alan Cole, *Exodus Tyndale Old Testament Commentary* (IVP, 1973), p.121.

3

Lord of laws, or God of gaps?

More years ago than I like to calculate, I was a hopeful science student in a grammar school sixth form. The master chiefly responsible for instructing us in the mysteries of A-level botany and zoology was something of a philosopher. J.B. Huxley seemed to be his apostle, George Bernard Shaw his high priest, and H.G. Wells his popular evangelist. These were heady days for materialists when, with a logic that escapes me, the incredible outbreak of human bestiality, self-destruction and carnage of the recent Second World War had persuaded many people of man's innate perfectibility, and his potential for hauling himself up by his own shoe-laces. Secularism was the order of the day, and our science master taught it (intermingled with the biology curriculum) with the fervour of a missionary. Second only to his enthusiasm for mankind was his contempt for every idea of God and the supernatural. The presence of a handful of evangelical students added fuel to his zeal. His attacks on us did us a world of good.

I recall how he dismissed the whole concept of order in nature (our argument for a creator), by invoking the unlimited possibilities of coincidence. As long as you give it enough time, absolutely anything can happen as a product of averages.

'Imagine a million monkeys, each with a typewriter', he

said one day. 'Imagine that each monkey rattles its paws totally at random over the keys. Given enough time, enough billions of years, one of those monkeys will eventually produce the complete works of Shakespeare, purely by accident.'

In a striking and oversimplified manner, the man was combining many of the typical ideas which lie behind so-called scientific attacks on belief in the Creator. Suggesting inconceivably large numbers of years and inconceivably large areas of space, you can imagine almost anything happening with no purpose in it, and no need for awkward purpose-sounding explanations. I'm grateful to that teacher. He cast so much light on the irrationality and chaos and perversity of a world which wants to dethrone its Creator. The world is being run by a bunch of monkeys with typewriters. It figures!

Now my schoolmaster of long ago may be an unfair example. But in all fairness, many of the 'scientific' objections to God and the supernatural are of no higher quality. 'The Bible is full of miracles, and science has proved that miracles are impossible'…something very like that is often trotted out with great sincerity, not by avowed atheists, but by ordinary average people who are afflicted with a vague idea that modern knowledge somehow favours unbelief. In actual fact the Bible is *not* 'full of miracles', as we shall see. A few patches admittedly deal very largely with miracles, and when they do so, 'modern science' is largely irrelevant. A miracle is, (let us say for the moment) a suspension of 'normal' laws of nature. Then the mere fact that we now know rather more about some of those laws, by no kind of logic leads us to be sure that they cannot be broken. A good policeman knows a great deal more about the laws of the land than does the average citizen. There can be few policemen whose knowledge has led them to the certainty that they cannot be broken. A sensible devotee of hang-gliding will have studied the law of gravity with more attention than most people. His extra knowledge of that law leads, not to the supposition that it cannot be broken, but to the certainty that it can be suspended for a while.

An equally persistent idea is often claimed as an objection to a controlling creator, rather than to special miracles. 'It used to be supposed that God was needed as an explanation of things which men could not understand. Now that we know so much about how things work, we can see that there is no need for a creator'. So the argument goes. Again it is a fallacy. Science has indeed taught us a good deal about how things work. But that in no way answers the question, '*Why* do they work like that?' *How* is not *why*. Only a fool would imagine that he has explained the 'why' of Eric Liddell's life, witness and death (the hero of *Chariots of Fire*) by describing how the ligaments and muscles in his legs worked. Does that explain *why* he set his heart on the Paris Olympics, *why* he refused to run on Sunday, and *why* he went to China as a missionary? And only a very determined materialist really thinks that he has plumbed the depths of the mystery of prayer, by explaining how many muscles are involved in the exercise of kneeling.

Unfortunately, there came a time when, quailing unnecessarily before the advance of scientific knowledge, some well-meaning believers in God took refuge in *the gaps in that knowledge*. 'Very well', they argued, 'clever men solve more and more mysteries of the universe. But always there is more to discover; always there are gaps in the knowledge; always things which cannot be explained. *That is where God comes in*. He is the explanation of the things which never *can* be explained.'

This is a thoroughly unworthy idea. It puts a premium on ignorance rather than faith. It pushes God further and further out of his own universe. It makes faith an enemy of knowledge. It frames the whole picture of belief in God in a context of constant retreat. Every new discovery dislodges him from another position. There is no room for the God of the gaps, in sensible Christian thinking, for this is simply not the God of whom the Bible speaks. There, God meets men at the centre of life, at the points of deepest significance, not out on the borders. Whatever answer the Christian gives to secularist arguments, he must insist on lifting his own concepts of God (and those of his opponents) to a higher level.

Big God and little images

Your God is too Small[1] is the title of a popular and perceptive book by the Christian writer J.B. Phillips, published shortly after the Second World War. He was complaining of shoddy and inadequate ideas of God which prevailed both among Christian believers and unbelievers. So often the arguments 'for' and 'against' are futile because they start from wrong premises. Naive Christians can try to defend positions which are indefensible because they are concepts of God never taught in the Bible. Their God is too small. More often the unbeliever attacks ideas which he rightly rejects, but wrongly imagines the Christian to hold. Even more often the non-Christian objects to concepts which are indeed truly Christian, but are simply gibberish to him because he is standing in the wrong position from which to view them correctly. *His* concept of *their* God is too small.

So we have statements like, 'A God of love would never punish anyone' – a suggestion which no thoughtful parent would apply to himself. Or it is said, 'I cannot believe that the Father would send any of his children to everlasting hell'. To which the answer is, 'he won't, not his *children*'. Someone else claims, 'If there were a God he would not allow...so-and-so'. They say it without giving a thought to the opposite implications. How does God *not* allow so-

and-so, whilst at the same time permitting people to be truly human and truly responsible, rather than puppets on a string or robots worked at the press of a button? Many objections to Christian belief should really be prefaced by the phrase…'If I were God…', which is self-cancelling.

Unfortunately believers can make similar mistakes. When God forbad the making of images (in the Second Commandment) he included in that ban the making of *images of himself*. The very people on whom he imposed the ban were doing it within days (Exodus 32). They got some gold rings together to represent high value. They shaped a bull to symbolize power and fertility. For good measure they make it a bull calf to speak of youth and vitality. With the cheerful consent of Moses' brother they set it up as an object of worship and announced '*These* are your gods… who brought you up out of the land of Egypt!' (Exodus 32:4) They had made God in their own image.

Tragically, the image was grossly misleading: all images are. That is why they are forbidden. A golden bull-calf may symbolize youth, strength and high value. It certainly does not symbolize holiness, authority, compassion, mercy or morality. It says nothing about some of the most vital attributes of God. In fact it actually misleads. It speaks of crude ideas of fertility-magic and animism. It echoes the frantic mysteries of corrupt Canaanite cults. Because the image was wrong the 'worship' quickly degenerated. Moses smashed their idol and made them (literally) eat it (verse 20).

Sadly, it is easy to make the same mistake. J.B. Phillips listed some of the inadequate, misleading ideas with which even well-meaning people surround the word 'God'. They put him in a box, restricting his wisdom and love to their own sectarian interests or mental horizons. They treat him as an umbrella under which to hide when life is tough. They imagine him as a bearded figure in the sky. They invest him with their own limitations. Phillips tried a little test. He asked a group of Christians whether, in their opinion, God understood radar (then a recent invention). Many of them instinctively said no – and then realized the absurdity of it. God taken aback at a new discovery!

The whole issue of the miraculous in Christianity has been befogged by this kind of small thinking about God. Friends and enemies of the faith have alike succumbed to it, though with quite different motives. The unbeliever, of course, rejects the supernatural and the miraculous, because its very possibility is a threat to him. 'The fact that men today do not find the biblical idea of God credible is nothing new – the majority of them never have'. In the closing decades of the twentieth century he will eagerly seize on 'science' as a stick with which to beat the supernatural. But the only thing new is the choice of stick (perhaps only the shape of the stick).

Lost in space
When in 1961 Yuri Gagarin returned triumphantly from the first manned space-flight he caused quite a sensation. 'I have been in the heavens and I did not see God', he announced. It was all splendid stuff and he spoke as a good obliging Communist. But there is no objective value in the remark. The men who actually landed on the moon claimed that they *did* see God, or at any rate, that they experienced him as they gazed at his creation. One of them has since become an evangelist. What you see depends on where you are standing: mentally and morally.

One can reply to Gagarin in the same semi-humorous vein in which he presumably spoke. There are many possible reasons why he might have travelled in the heavens without seeing God. Perhaps God was somewhere else at the time; space is really very big and Gagarin did not travel very far after all. Perhaps God was so big that the Russian could not see him. That is perfectly logical. Presumably the spider on a window-sill of a skyscraper does not 'see' the skyscraper; it is his whole world. Perhaps Gagarin was travelling too fast to understand what he saw; you cannot 'see' the porter on a rural railway platform if the train passes at 100 m.p.h. A rocket goes a good deal faster.

Of course these are not serious replies, though they probably typify the inadequate ideas of God which some believers and some unbelievers embrace. The true answers are much higher and deeper. Gagarin was no nearer to God and no further away from him in space than on earth. God was with him when he entered the capsule, with him at the highest curve of his parabola in space, and waiting to meet him in Siberia when he returned. For 'in him we live and move and have our being' (Acts 17:28). He did not see God because God is invisible spirit, and because unless a man is spiritually reborn he cannot see or understand anything about God. The Creator does not occupy one spot in space to the exclusion of any other spot. Quite specifically the heavens cannot contain him (*see* 1 Kings 8:27). Ironically, the atheistic space-pioneer who survived the dangers of that epic journey without seeing God, soon afterwards lost his life in a car crash, and met God, as we all must. '...it is appointed for men to die once, and after that comes judgment' (Hebrews 9:27).

No room for God?

It is time to look at the discussion rather more seriously.

The argument goes something like this. Science has given us a totally new picture of the universe which leaves no room for God and no need for God . It shows the vast process of space and time which is simply going on of its own accord and the laws which govern that process. It is a totally interlocking system which provides for itself and explains itself. Everything that happens is because of something else that happens; every effect has a cause and every cause leads to an effect: everything is fixed. Water

35

boils at 100^0. Snowflakes crystallize at an angle of 60^0. Every planet is on a mathematical course. In a splendid Victorian yarn the author can picture explorers overawing the simple natives by declaring that in five minutes' time there would be an eclipse of the sun. The impressive fulfilment of their forecast was not due to an intervention on their behalf and certainly did not prove that they were gods. It expressed the fact that they knew the laws of nature, and they knew how they worked.

Now such a picture provided by science gives us, it is claimed, an explanation of everything. It has no need for God. Or at the very most it can make room for a God who may have started everything off in the first place but certainly not a 'living God' who interferes, intervenes, answers prayers and makes things happen. The Bible tells us the story of a drought that came to the land of Israel as a consequence of the prayers and protestations of the prophet Elijah. Two years later when the people repent and turn back to God, Elijah goes up on the cliff and prays for rain. He sees a cloud appearing like a man's hand, and continues to pray. Before long the desperately needed rain has arrived. But science tells us that rain falling on Mount Carmel that day was the consequence of unalterable laws which interlink back and back and back; in a sense the very beginning of all weather brought the guarantee that it would rain on that particular day in that particular place. The rain was brought by a wind from the Mediterranean, the wind blew from the Mediterranean because of particular changes in pressure, possibly over the Atlantic. These came into conflict with the different pressures existing over the Arabian desert. That system owed its origin to atmospheric events which took place the year before. Those events were again dependent on previous events the year before that; and so on, so the argument goes. Elijah's prayer must have been either a lucky break or was based on slightly more knowledge of prevailing weather conditions than that possessed by the general public. One thing which could not have affected it was prayer. The process of events was already marching and could not be altered.

Now all of this is very attractive and very persuasive. It is attractive because it appeals to modern man's proud conviction that he knows a great deal more than anyone has ever known before. It is persuasive because science so obviously *works*. Everything around us from medicine to motorcars, from computers to cassettes, from telephones to television sets, is a practical expression of the outworking of scientific principles. The theories have been proved in practice over and over again; the thing works so the theory must be true.

In actual fact, this impressive argument is full of the most enormous fallacies. It confuses proven theory which has led to applied science, with a particular philosophy which continues to be pure theory. When a scientist seeks to answer the question 'how?' we must listen to him with considerable respect, for that is the task and the right of science. But when a scientist attempts to answer the question 'why?' or 'who?', then he has stopped being a scientist and is claiming to be a philosopher or even a theologian. In that case when he speaks he has no more authority than, say, a greengrocer, a steeplejack or a car mechanic. He has a good deal *less* authority than a poet, a philosopher or a clergyman. When a particular scientist says, 'I believe that the whole universe is a closed mechanistic system, in which everything that happens is explained by everything else that happens in one self-dependent unity', he is not expressing an inescapable fact, but is quoting an interesting theory.

When another scientist who is a Christian (and there are plenty of them) quotes the same marvellous collection of observed facts and goes on to say, 'Here I see marvellous illustrations of the fact that the God whom I worship is in control of all things, and in him they live and move and have their being', then as far as the facts of scientific research are concerned, he stands intellectually at exactly the same level as his unbelieving colleague. Both of them are expressing their belief. Both of them are taking a very real step of faith. In fact, unbelief requires the acceptance by faith of a great number of things that are very hard to credit!

I remember, years ago, watching an appearance on television of Sir Bernard Lovell, who was at that time Director of the Jodrell Bank Radio Telescope Research Project. He listened with courtesy and respect to a believing scientist and an unbelieving scientist arguing with each other about the basis of their faith. When the interviewer turned to him and asked his own opinion as to whether the facts of scientific discovery supported faith or unbelief, he replied quite simply. 'The facts have very little to do with the argument on either side. I find that believing scientists are impressed by what they regard as illustrations of the activity of God, and unbelieving scientists are equally impressed by what they see as illustrations of a universe functioning without God. In both cases the actual scientific facts are not evidences at all, but are simply illustrations of a position that is taken up for quite different reasons.'

Law and order

In actual fact the whole impressive picture which science gives us of an integrated and self-supporting unity given by natural laws, presents the atheist with at least as many problems as it presents the Christian, probably far more. The very word 'law' which the scientist constantly uses is in itself a very awkward give-away. One normally assumes law comes from a law-giver. Similar language constantly creeps into use especially in popular versions of scientific subjects. Phrases like 'nature's answer', 'nature's provision', and words like 'adapt', 'planned', 'patterned' – all of these phrases come uncomfortably close to implying a law-giver, an architect, a planner *etc*. Of course the scientist may hotly reply that he is simply using popular phrases, even slightly poetic phrases, to enable himself to describe what he is dealing with. The interesting thing is that he keeps finding himself compelled to use words that imply intelligence, purpose and a mind.

The impressive fact, very often ignored or forgotten nowadays, is that the earliest scientists, who were the real pioneers, deliberately used words like 'law' because this is precisely how they saw it. The earliest motivation for modern science was almost totally Christian. 'It was not until certain specific Christian attitudes were added to the background of pre-Christian philosophy that science as we know it really got under way.'[2] As a matter of plain historical fact science originally grew up in Christian soil. Bacon, Newton, Pascal, Descartes, Kepler, Rutherford; all of these men drew the very possibility of the scientific method from the medieval insistence on the rationality of God.

'Ah well, they were bound to be Christians, because everyone was a Christian at that time. They were simply children of their own generation and naturally expressed their science in naive theological terms', someone may reply. But it is much more fundamental than that. They built the very rationale (that leads to the possibility of modern science based on a collection and interpretation of facts, allied to the assumption that those same facts will go on repeating themselves in the same predictable way) precisely on their belief that a world created by a rational God will, in fact, behave rationally. The pioneer members of the Royal Society would have been astonished at the suggestion that an ordered universe excludes the possibility of the supernatural. It was precisely their faith in a supernatural-personal-rational God which led them to look for order and to speak of laws. 'The rise of modern science does not conflict with what the Bible teaches;

indeed at a crucial point the scientific revolution rested on what the Bible teaches.'[3] A scientist as distinguished (and as contemporary) as Albert Einstein made the very same point. Though this is not always realized, his 'theory of relativity' does not in fact make everything relative, but is based on the assumption that there is totally constant law in every part of the universe. 'I cannot believe that God plays dice with the cosmos', said Einstein.[4]

Precisely. The ordered universe whose continued order and predictability is a *sine qua non* for any scientific thinking, finds its order and its predictability in its source: God who is rational, wise and sovereign. In a remarkable word picture, one of the psalmists makes this point.

> For ever, O LORD, thy word
>> is firmly fixed in the heavens....
>> thou hast established the earth, and it stands fast.
> By thy appointment they stand this day;
>> for all things are thy servants (Psalm 119:89–91).

The writer is putting together a lyrical praise of God's Word. He turns from the Bible to the observed world for an illustration. Look at this world of order, he is saying. Look at the vastness of the universe. See the *law* that runs through it all. Why? Because God made it that way, and runs it that way. How? By speaking the creative word. At the beginning all things sprang into being at his command. 'God said, "Let there be light"; and there was light.... God said, "Let the waters...be gathered together...". And it was so....' *etc.* (Genesis 1). Now, the psalmist reasons magnificently, the same *Word* which brought worlds into being is the Word that is announced in commandments, precepts and laws, in other words *the Bible*.

> The heavens declare Thy glory, Lord,
> In every star Thy wisdom shines;

But when our eyes behold Thy Word,
We read Thy name in fairer lines.
(Isaac Watts)

...And my life too is fashioned and guided by the same hands that beckoned the stars and the flowers at the world's dawning, and made the day and the night. (Helmut Thielicke)[5]

When is a law not a law?
Look again at these laws of nature which scientists find so necessary and yet so irritating to talk about. There are three possible ways of regarding these 'laws'. First of all they may be 'mere brute facts' as C.S. Lewis puts it. That is the way that many of the atheistic scientists prefer to regard them. What we are handling and observing are simply collections of facts which are overwhelmingly numerous and all seem to say the same thing. 'This is simply how it is.' They are not 'laws' at all in the sense of coming from a law-giver or having a purpose. They simply express things; they indisputably exist. If that is so, then the existence of these 'laws' does not prove an argument against God and the supernatural at all. They even cast doubt on the possibility of valid scientific thinking, because such thinking depends totally on the assumption that things will keep on happening the way they have been observed to happen. But why in that case should they need to be irreversible and predictable? What guarantee is there that they will keep on happening?

The second possible explanation is that the apparent 'laws' are merely the application of the law of averages. Again there are many thinkers who believe that this is so. Everybody knows that the longer you toss a coin indiscriminately, the more nearly 'heads' and 'tails' will come up equal. This does not imply that somebody is making it happen; in fact it implies the very opposite. This is simply

41

how averages work out. So, the argument goes, science presents us with apparent 'laws' which are simply the statement of the averages of vast numbers of experiments and observations. But here again this is not an argument against the existence of an outside source of influence (such as God). Nor does it begin to give any explanation of *why* things happen according to these averages. Nor (once more) do they provide any logical guarantee that averages will continue to perform in the same predictable way in the future.

The third possible explanation is that scientific 'laws' in fact are stating necessary truths. *In the very nature of things,* this is how it must be. In that case they are true and necessary in exactly the same way that mathematics gives us what is true and necessary. Two plus two always equals four. It is in the very nature of things and cannot be any different. There is no need to ask, 'why?'. That would be like asking, 'Why is a fact a fact?' But again this offers no convincing argument against belief in someone 'out there' who has created things precisely to be as they are. The statement 'things must be as they are', contains within it something that sounds very like morality and logic. But whose morality? Whose logic?

The biblical answer

Now to all of this the Bible gives a splendid, clear and bold answer. *The universe is not ruled by law; it is ruled by God.* The 'laws' are simply helpful ways of expressing the principles by which God rules his created universe. From beginning to end the Bible is full of this statement, and even more often than it is stated it is simply assumed. The Bible begins with an announcement sublime in its simplicity. 'In the beginning God created the heavens and the earth.' Everything that exists is seen as coming from the purpose of God expressed in his created word. 'God said, "Let there be light"; and there was light' (Genesis 1:3). As the psalmist says, 'He spoke and it was done,' (Psalm 33:9). The superb account then goes on to tell us very little of *how* God created all things. It is as mistaken to imagine the first chapter of Genesis tells us the *how* of astronomy, biology and physics, as it is to imagine that astronomers, biologists and physicists answer the questions *why* and *who?*.

The Bible then goes on to speak equally positively of God as governing and creating the universe which he originally made. '...upholding the universe by his word of power' (Hebrews 1:3). He gives the light, the rain and the seasons. He forms the mountains and creates the winds. He made the constellations and he now brings the daily dawn. Snow, frost, ice, winds and waters all obey him. Intriguingly, in the light of our last chapter, he orders the rise and fall of the Nile (*see* Psalm 147:15–18; Amos 4:13; 5:8; 9:5–6; Acts 14:15–17). And so the Bible goes on. The chemical world, the vegetable world, the world of irrational creatures, and the world of rational mankind is all governed by the God in whom 'we live and move and have our being' (Acts 17:28). In these and many other Scriptures the writer is clearly regarding God as the first cause, and equally clearly has little or no interest in second causes, though that does not deny that the second causes exist. It is the second causes which we conveniently call the laws of nature and they take their very existence from the fact that they are expressions of the first cause himself. The abstract conceptions of space and time, nature, the cosmos are all alien to the Hebrew mind since the sovereignty of God is absolute and nothing exists without him.

Calvin has suggested that the mode of God's government varies according to the nature of the thing which he is governing. So he rules inanimate objects by what we observe as chemical and physical laws. He rules the vegetable world by the outworking of what we call organic laws. He rules animals by the employment of instinct which is a 'higher' law. Unconverted men bring us higher still, so that intelligence and choice are employed as the instruments of God's rule without of course interfering with the genuineness of their will and responsibility. Highest of all, the converted man is ruled by God through the instrument of his own willing obedience and dedication. *Thus the whole dichotomy in our western minds between 'natural' and 'supernatural' simply does not exist in Hebrew and biblical thinking.* Everything is 'natural' in that it expresses the laws which God has built into his creation. Everything is 'supernatural' in that it expresses in one way or another the sovereign rule of God. 'If God is active in any part of the physical world, he is in all. If the divine activity means anything, then *all* the events of what we call the physical world are dependent on that activity.'[6] So says Professor MacKay. R. T. France says the same thing when he writes, 'Let it be firmly stated and squarely faced up to that the Bible from Genesis to Revelation is stiff with supernatural ideas and language.'[7]

C.S. Lewis presents the whole argument in his usual splendid way in an article entitled *The Laws of Nature*. This was later incorporated in his classic book *Miracles*.[8] He takes the illustration of a billiard table standing in the saloon of a large ship. He shows how the law of physics decrees that when one billiard ball sets another billiard ball in motion the momentum lost by the first ball exactly equals the momentum gained by the second.

How or Why?
This is a simple illustration of one of the 'laws of nature'. But of course it only explains *how things happen*. It does nothing towards explaining *why* it happens which is what advocates of a mechanistic self-explanatory universe constantly imagine that it does. Lewis points out the law is indisputedly true but it simple does not *make anything happen* to the balls. As far as the law stands alone the billiard balls will never begin to move. To get them to move, a

man must strike them with a billiard cue. Or the ship needs to hit a particularly big wave which causes it to lurch and tilt the table. In that case a law did not cause the billiard balls to move but simply expresses the fact that when they move (for some other reason) they will move according to the laws of physics. 'The dazzlingly obvious conclusion now arose in my mind, in the whole history of the universe the laws of nature have never produced a single event. They are the pattern to which every event must conform, provided only that it can be induced to happen. But how do you get it to do that? How do you get a move on? ....Up to now I had had a vague idea that the laws of nature could make things happen. I now saw that this was exactly like thinking that you could increase your income by doing sums about it. The *laws* are the pattern to which events conform: the source of events must be sought elsewhere.'[8]

In other words we are back to the same old argument again. Scientific observation and the laws of nature do not explain why and who at all; they simply explain how. I ask 'Why is my wife angry with me?' It is irritating only to be told as an answer, 'because adrenalin is flowing from her pituitary gland.' That is *how* but I am no nearer knowing *why*. The actual *why* is in fact 'because it is our anniversary and I've forgotten.' The pituitary gland is, if you like, part of the closed system. But my forgetfulness is the fact from outside that is really important and really gives the explanation. And my forgetfulness can be atoned for by another fact from outside. I can buy her some flowers.

Divine law-breaker?

Now of course the really alert atheist can listen to this whole argument so far and if he does not like it (and being an atheist he cannot possibly like it) then at this stage he can shift his ground. 'It is all very well to talk about God employing the laws of nature as his instruments', he will reply. 'But your Bible says very much more than that. You Christians claim not only that God invisibly rules the universe in ways which by their very nature can neither be proved or disproved, but also you will persist in claiming that God constantly *interferes* with the course of nature. If the Bible story were simply an account of how God invisibly rules his creation, then all that would be needed would be the first chapter of Genesis and perhaps a few psalms thrown in that express the same fact in slightly more poetic language. But the story does not end there. Your God is constantly intervening in special and supernatural ways. He does not settle for ordinary clouds and rain but supernaturally drowns the world in the time of Noah. Not content with inviting mankind to admire his rule over nature, he positively invites mankind to alter the course of things by praying to him. What your Bible really describes is not a God who makes natural laws but the God who *breaks* natural laws.'

And of course in a sense he is perfectly right. 'It is no good pretending... when we speak to God that we *are* introducing a whole realm of thought quite alien to the secular way of seeing things. We *are* talking about a supernatural, transcendent, personal, interfering God, and there is nothing to be gained by trying to camouflage the fact.'[9] It is here that the whole argument between a 'closed system' and an 'open system' joins battle. A closed system is totally self-explanatory, self-supporting and interrelated and can by its very nature allow no outside interference. Indeed nothing 'outside' can possibly exist by definition since the closed system is by definition the whole of existence. Just because the naturalist thinks that nothing but nature exists, the word nature means to him merely everything, or the whole show, or whatever there is. And if that is what we mean by nature, then of course nothing else exists. This is the impression given by the Greek word for nature 'physis' and the Latin 'natura'. This is why the word nature is in fact so popular with atheists who hold to a totally closed system. It is 'a vast process in space and time which is going on of its own accord' and of course in that extreme sense *nothing* in the Bible thinking can be termed as 'natural' since by definition nothing goes on of its own accord. God alone is the first cause. Without him nothing would ever exist, let alone 'work'.[10]

On the other hand, the concept of an 'open system' denies that the universe is in itself totally self-explanatory and self-dependent. It is open to the constant possibility of intervention from 'outside'. James Houston has listed four attributes of an open system. First it has various possibilities for unpredictable change. Secondly the future is not totally determined by the present condition. Thirdly the system is open to relationships with other systems. Fourthly the final condition will be different from the original state.[11]

Now of course the two views are totally at war with each other and although the idea of miracles, answers to prayer and intervention of God, may seem to bring the argument on to a different level, they are really simply projections of the claim that God rules his universe by means of the laws of nature. For the simple observable fact is that the laws of nature are constantly being interfered with or altered without there being any logical or moral impossibility involved. Take a simple example. A mother out in the garden sees her child beginning to fall from a high upstairs window. The law of gravity says that he surely will be dashed to the ground. The laws of biology say that as a consequence he will certainly die. But the mother says 'no'. She rushes beneath the falling child to catch him and break his fall. She lays him on the ground and staggers to get help. The hospital which can give the necessary help is miles away. The laws which govern space and time say that she cannot possibly shout across those miles. But she finds a telephone and does just that. The doctor is eager to help. But laws of nature say that he can walk at only three miles per hour. Undeterred, he jumps into a car and drives at twenty times that speed. He finds the child is bleeding and a grim law says that he will bleed to death. But the doctor has blood plasma with him. So we could go on. Again and again the laws of nature have said one thing but without in any way offending those laws or producing a moral and logical absurdity, we have altered them – defied them if you wish – simply by bringing other laws to bear upon them. If a loving mother can do this, cannot a loving God do it? He can and he does. The world is full of examples of his ability and his willingness to answer prayers, to meet needs, to guide lives, and most of all to change hearts and to save souls.

So as a matter of simple observation and experience, we do *not* live in a closed system. We live in a system that is constantly being interfered with by someone from 'outside'. For man himself is outside of a mechanistic system. He must be because he can change its mechanism. The room in which the reader of this book sits and peruses it contents is full of illustrations of that reader's defiance or alteration or use of the laws of nature 'from outside'. The book itself is very likely the product of the nature of a tree being fundamentally changed. So is the table at which he sits and reads. If it is growing dark there is nothing inevitable in the sun's onward march which makes it impossible for him to continue to read. He switches on an electric light. Laws of nature may well decree that he is unavoidably short-sighted. But this makes little trouble for him since he employs a pair of spectacles. The clothes which he wears are the result of a quite drastic alteration in the nature of some other object. The meal, after his reading session, will almost certainly involve processes of freezing, tinning, thawing and cooking, which to an unsophisticated dweller in some parts of the world, would appear constant miracles.

If a human being can constantly perform these 'miracles', then how can it be impossible or immoral or unreasonable for God to perform what indeed are truly miracles? In 'ordinary' events God works providentially through his government of natural laws. In more miraculous and supernatural events God continues to act; perhaps by suspending one law of nature in favour of another, or causing one law of nature to supervene upon another. The divine act of miracle is not an act of suspending the pattern to which events conform, but of feeding new events into that pattern. The plagues of Egypt which we have already examined gave a particularly striking example of this fact. The ordinary misfortunes which befall the area and which include within them very considerable advantages too (such as the annual rising of the Nile) illustrate God's rule in 'natural' events.

The disasters which fell upon Egypt at a particular time and in particular circumstances, when God was rescuing his people from the clutches of a tyrant, illustrate the speeding up or the intensification of these same natural laws to produce what we then call a supernatural event or a miracle. 'A miracle is emphatically not an event without cause or without results. Its cause is the activity of God: its results follow according to natural law.' ... 'In calling them miracles we do not mean that they are contradictions or outrages; we mean that, left to her own resources, nature could never produce them.'[12] And as a matter of fact 'left to her own resources', nature cannot ever produce anything, even the *natural*. Or so the Bible teaches and so the Christian believes. There is certainly absolutely nothing within true scientific knowledge and discovery to contradict that belief.

Nor is there any need for the Christian to be apologetic and half-ashamed of his doctrine of God. Least of all need he have resource to the 'god of the gaps'. It is the living God with whom we have to deal. He is, amongst other

49

things, the Lord of nature. And precisely because he is the Lord of nature, he is also the Lord of the supernatural.

Notes for chapter three

[1] J.B. Phillips, *Your God is too Small* (Epworth Press, 1956).
[2] A.N. Triton, *Whose World?* (IVP, 1970).
[3] Francis Schaeffer, *How Should We Then Live?* (Fleming H. Revell 1976), p.132.
[4] 'London Observer', 5th April 1964.
[5] Helmut Thielicke, *How the World Began* (James Clarke & Co, 1964), p.33.
[6] D.M. MacKay, *The Clockwork Image* (IVP, 1974), p.57.
[7] R.T. France, *The Living God* (IVP, 1970), p.120.
[8] C.S. Lewis, *Miracles* (Fontana, 1960).
[9] D.M. MacKay, *The Clockwork Image* (IVP, 1974) p.121.
[10] C.S. Lewis, *Miracles* (Fontana, 1960).
[11] James Houston, *I Believe in the Creator* (Hodder, 1979).
[12] So argues C.S. Lewis again in *Miracles*.
Compare Augustine – 'How can anything be against nature that happens by the will of God, since the will of so great a Creator is the nature of every made thing?' (*City of God* 12:8,2).

4

'The Bible's full of it'

In my open-air preaching days, the frequent encounters
with 'hecklers' provided a good deal of humour, helped to
gather a crowd, and provided useful insights into the way
people's minds work when they are really determined not
to believe in God. An old tag which I cannot trace often
came to mind.

> Behold, how many things hard to credit one must
> believe, in order not to be a Christian.

A persistent idea was abroad that the Bible is 'full of contradictions'. Asked to explain these, I used to invite the
questioner to show me one. I would hand him my Bible
helpfully. He would finger it nervously, ruffle a few pages,
and then often retort, 'Well it's full of them!'

'All the easier to find one if there are so many,' I would
respond, perhaps a little unkindly. He would turn a few
more pages and give it up, pulling one out of the air or
from some confused memory. For of course it is simply
not true that the Bible is full of them. The occasional difficulty or seeming contradiction, yes. But *full* of them?

A similar illusion afflicts people when they think about
miracles. 'The Bible is full of *them* too: miracles on every
page. Of course the writers didn't understand science in
those days. We know *better* now.'

But is the Bible really crowded with miracles? If we stick rigidly to the word translated so in the Authorized Version, a glance at a Bible concordance will reveal a surprisingly small use of the word.

'Now you are playing tricks with words', our critic will reply. 'You know very well that the Old Testament is full of references to God's intervention, to his suspension of nature, to his reversal of the way in which things will normally happen.'

But is it really so? Imitate my heckler-friends, and try thumbing through the pages of the Bible, looking at random for that kind of event. You may be surprised how long you take to find one, if you genuinely turn the pages at random. Of course there is a cluster of them in the Exodus story, as we have seen. The book provides us with some useful synonyms and sets us on the path of a definition. We shall return to it.

After that, what? Apart from a few remarkable provisions in the desert, the story carries us on to the borders of Canaan and the books of Joshua and Judges. Some incidents are calculated to raise an eyebrow, but how many of these are truly miraculous? The Israelites cross the flooded Jordan and find it no barrier. There is the same uncanny mixture of 'natural' and 'supernatural' that we have noticed in Egypt. The timing is God's.

'Command the priests who bear the ark..."when you come to the brink of the waters... stand still"' (Joshua 3:8).

But the instrument is 'natural'.

'The waters coming down from above stood and rose up in a heap ...beside Zarethan, and those flowing down toward the ...Salt Sea, were wholly cut off'(Joshua 3:16).

Travellers have described similar incidents in the same area.[1] A land-slip caused the high sandy banks of the Jordan, undermined by flood waters, to collapse and block the water running from the north, which accordingly 'rose up in a heap' to the north, and 'flowed down to the Salt

Sea' in the south. 'To accept that explanation does not detract in any way from the supernatural intervention which opened the way to Israel just at the moment when they needed to cross.'[2]

There quickly follows the marvellous story of the collapse of the walls of Jericho. The same features are there again. The method employed is God's command. The timing coincides perfectly. The event itself is rare, but not supernatural. Today's ruins of Old Testament Jericho are a little enigmatic in their evidence, but one can certainly see cheap and unstable mud-bricks from Joshua's time superimposed on much more solid stone ruins from a thousand years earlier; not the best kind of security. The next startling event is really mind-blowing at first sight. In a running battle through the valleys and across the hills just north of Jerusalem,

> Joshua ... said in the sight of Israel,
> 'Sun, stand thou still at Gibeon,
> and thou Moon in the valley of Aijalon.'
> And the sun stood still, and the moon stayed,
> until the nation took vengeance on their enemies.
> (Joshua 10:12–13)

However, this does not really require the suspension of the earth's rotation. What Joshua needed was not a longer day but a longer night. To be more explicit, he needed a delayed dawn to exploit the advantage of his ambush, when he 'came upon them suddenly, having marched up all night from Gilgal' (Joshua 10:9). Now it was dawn: the sun stood low in the east over Gibeon, and the moon in the west over Aijalon. The required darkness was prolonged by a violent hailstorm which actually caused more deaths in the murky confusion than had the first breaking of the ambush (Joshua 10:11). A student friend has described how she camped in the valley of Aijalon and had her tent knocked down and damaged by just such a morning storm. No astounding interruption of the earth's rotation is needed to interpret the story,[3] meet the need, and fulfil Joshua's poetic prayer, which can be translated equally well as....

> Be eclipsed, O sun in Gibeon
> And thou moon in the valley of Aijalon.

The story is very much the same for the rest of the Old Testament. Where are the miracles 'on every page' in the stories of the Judges, of the great prophet Samuel, of the long and hectic life of David himself? There are some notable feats in battle, and some remarkable casualty figures. But no more remarkable than, say, those for the Battle of Crecy, in which the French lost twelve thousand and the English forty dead, with French forces outnumbering English by three to one. It is well known that both the British Second World War General, Orde Wingate, and the modern Israeli hero, Moshe Dayan, modelled much of their strategy on the details from these Old Testament books.

There is surprisingly little of the miraculous in the lives of the prophets whose ministries were contemporary with the great historical books of the Bible. Except, of course, the mystery of prophecy itself. Again and again activities and events are attributed to 'the Lord'. This is fully in accord with the biblical teaching that God rules and over-rules at all times. But miracles as they are popularly understood are very hard to find.

A notable exception is that of the successive ministries of Elijah and Elisha. Here the striking intervention of God abounds. Under Elijah, [4] the note of judgment predominates; God strikes down the nation with drought and famine for embracing corrupt Baalism, he marvellously provides for his prophet during the judgment period, and then throws the nation to its knees in repentance when fire pours down from heaven. Elisha's adventures [5] speak more of God's grace and mercy, and most of them have a surprisingly 'homely' touch about them. A water-supply is purified, oil is provided without limit, breath restores a dead child, bread and fruit feed a hundred men, and immersion in the water of Jordon brings cleansing to a leper. These are curious and suggestive forerunners of Christ's miracles.

Pieces in perspective

Now in all of this, is there not a pattern? The penetrating Benjamin Warfield has said, 'Miracles do not appear on the page of Scripture vagrantly, here, there, and elsewhere indifferently, without assignable reason. They belong to revelation periods.'[6] Indeed they do. There are only two great clusters of miracles. One, ushers in God's first calling to an imprisoned race to be the people of God; smashing the religious and political forces which oppressed them, bringing them out of slavery with signs and wonders, carrying them through desert wanderings where spiritual lessons were burned deep, and bringing them into a new land where his name would be venerated, his law preserved, his temple set up. The other, rescues the nation once more as it is in dire danger of submerging in a flood of superstition and immorality in which the very name of God could have been forgotten. If we count the experiences of Ezekiel and Daniel (recorded in the books so named) then again we have a turning-point, a climactic moment in the history of God's people when *their* history becomes 'revelation history'. Far from occupying 'every page', the Old Testament miracles occupy very few, and their appearance has a clear reason.

Is the same pattern discernible in the New Testament? Before we pursue that subject we must pause to analyse further just what the Old Testament means by the miraculous. Are there more clues there to its frequency and its purpose?

The Old Testament employs a number of Hebrew and Aramaic words to describe these activities of God which we normally think of as beyond nature. Each has very suggestive connotations.

There are wonderful actions. A cluster of words is drawn from the verb 'to be different'. In English they are usually translated *wonders*, and they suggest the reaction of those who witness them. God is 'terrible in glorious deeds, doing *wonders*' (Exodus 15:11. My italics. The immediate reference is the crossing of the Red Sea).

'Tomorrow the LORD will do *wonders* among you' (Joshua 3:5 My italics) promises Joshua, as the people prepare to cross the flooded Jordan river. Looking back to the one event and forward to the other, the aged Moses gives a classic description of God's marvellous acts. 'Has any god ever attempted to go and take a nation ... by trials, by signs, by *wonders*, and by war, by a mighty hand and an outstretched arm, and by great terrors ... that the Lord God did for you in Egypt before your eyes?' (Deuteronomy 4:34. My italics) 'Before your eyes'. Look with awe!

In a later 'revelation-crisis' for Israel (conquered, dragged into Babylonian captivity and in danger of lapsing into paganism) there comes a startling wonder. Their conqueror, a powerful tyrant (another Pharaoh, so to speak) has a disturbing dream. It defies the understanding of his magicians and when it is interpreted by Daniel it reveals God's opposition to pagan pride and arrogance. When the emperor has learned his bitter lesson he exclaims,

> How great are his signs,
>   how mighty his wonders!
> His kingdom is an everlasting
>   kingdom,

and his dominion is from
   generation to generation.
(Daniel 4:3)

A later tyrant is compelled to admit,

He delivers and rescues,
   he works signs and wonders
   in heaven and on earth,
he who has saved Daniel
   from the power of the lions.
(Daniel 6:27)

In these and similar incidents the word 'wonder' or 'wonderful' aptly sums up the amazed discovery of the onlooker as he observes God's powerful intervention.

There are mighty and powerful deeds. Recalling the Exodus story, the psalmist describes 'the mighty doings of the LORD' (Psalm 106:2). Another psalmist tells us

one generation shall laud thy works to another,
and shall declare thy mighty acts.
(Psalm 145:4)

and then goes on to celebrate the 'everlasting kingdom and dominion' of God, in terms exactly similar to the two quotations from the book of Daniel. But (and this is the really striking thing) what the psalmist is now speaking of is not the Exodus kind of event but 'natural' happenings in God's providence, such as providing food in season, giving protection from disaster and hearing the prayer of the suppliant. The same word is used to describe events as widely differing as the creation of the world, the destruction of an army, and an apparently chance meeting between a man and a girl.

There are meaningful and significant happenings. This cluster of words is usually translated as 'sign'. God asks complainingly of Israel in the wilderness, 'How long will they not believe in me, in spite of all the signs which I have wrought among them?'(Numbers 14:11). Much later Nehemiah looks back in prayer to those very times and speaks of the 'signs' and 'wonders' which were performed then 'against Pharaoh' (Nehemiah 9:10). The combination of the word 'sign' and the word 'wonder' is very common indeed, as if God were saying 'You will not make anything of the event which causes you to be startled and surprised until you learn to see its meaning and its significance.'

It is this emphasis on *revelation* that really marks out the Old Testament approach to miracles. 'Miracle, therefore, does not appear in particular as an event of the supernatural order, it is not characterized by the fact that it suspends the laws of nature: it is extraordinary because it manifests, generally in an unexpected manner, with a special intensity, the presence of God here below.'[7] The characteristic thing about a Bible miracle is that it reveals the presence of God.

This in turn leads to the *demand for faith*. The miracle does not simply draw attention to the truth by producing astonishment in the onlooker. The event is an essential part of what the truth is trying to convey. Both the outstanding act and the underlying truth which it portrays work together to produce and nourish faith.

Thus the LORD saved Israel that day from the hand of the Egyptians; and Israel saw the Egyptians dead upon the seashore. And Israel saw the great work which the LORD did against the Egyptians, and the people feared the LORD; and they believed in the LORD and in his servant Moses. (Exodus 14:31)

That says almost everything that the Old Testament miracle implies.

Where does the finger point?

So as Alan Richardson says, 'The biblical miracles must be discussed not merely *historically* (did they happen?) but also *philosophically* (what is their meaning?).'[8] A miracle is a finger pointing towards God, an exclamation mark in the sky, so to speak. It is perfectly possible to ignore the direction of the pointing finger, to turn the exclamation mark into a question mark. The faith is never automatic or compulsory. There is always another possible explanation if you want to have one. When confronted with a 'sign' in the time of Isaiah, King Ahaz treated it with contempt and sarcasm (Isaiah 7:10–16). Struggling against the implications of a succession of devastating 'signs' Pharaoh simply hardened himself in unbelief. In the words of Martin-Achard, 'To those who do not believe in God, miracle reveals nothing.'[9]

Perhaps we are now in a position to get some overall view of the 'supernatural' in Old Testament times.

Its starting-place is in the Bible doctrine of creation. All things came into existence by God's command, and remain in being by his constant activity. Nature's 'laws' are an expression of that activity.

Theologically we can speak first of *God's sovereignty*. He rules all things as King and Lord.

> Whatever the LORD pleases he does,
> in heaven and on earth,
> in the seas and all deeps. (Psalm 135:6)

He does what he pleases! That exactly sums up the sovereignty of God. The psalmist goes on in the next verse to give as examples the rising of clouds, the flash of lightning, the downpour of rain and the blowing of the wind, 'from his storehouses'. He seems to be describing exactly the welcome onset of the wet winter in the land of Israel.

59

But in verse 8 he immediately goes on to quote as another example,

> He it was who smote the first-born of Egypt,
>   both of man and of beast;
> who in thy midst, O Egypt,
>   sent signs and wonders
>   against Pharaoh and all his servants.

We can also speak of his *providence,* that is the process by which God exercises his rule without contradicting the nature of that which he rules. His providence over living things, particularly over human beings, is a very complex subject. The book of Esther provides the classic biblical example of providence. Here we see an extraordinary series of events in which God never visibly appears nor is his name ever mentioned, nor does anyone ever engage in a specifically religious action. A girl wins a beauty contest, a man accidently hears a plot whispered outside a palace gate, a king has a restless night and begins to read a book to avoid boredom, a very nasty court character makes a particularly ludicrous mistake in conversation with the king; and out of all this God works to deliver the Jewish people from the danger of a pogrom. The events happened 'naturally' but God's will is achieved. Again there is no sharp distinction between natural and supernatural events. As Job says, God does 'marvelous things without number:' (Job 5:9) he brings rain, he causes the crops to grow, he sees to it that dishonesty fails, he undertakes mercy for orphans and protects the poor. So we have linked together without distinction, events in the natural world and the independent conscious moral decisions of men and women. Both kinds of events, though so different in their nature, are examples of the providence of God.

Thirdly, we can speak of God's *direct intervention*. He

works in such an obvious manner that men are astonished and caused to 'wonder'. God is seen to be pointing to himself in acts that become signs. Faith is demanded and an obedient response called for. The 'normal' is reversed or replaced by the unusual, the impressive, even the frightening *e.g.* when the fire fell in answer to Elijah's prayer as he confronted the prophets and priests of Baal, 'And when all the people saw it they fell on their faces; and they said, "The LORD, he is God". ' (1 Kings 18:36–40).

The question is not, 'How on earth did he do *that*?' Rather it is, 'What can I see of the power and grace of God in this? How must I react? What does he want of me?'

The right reaction

Before we leave the Old Testament we are still left to ask and answer a very important question. What is the life to which the observer of God's mighty works and the reader of his Word is called? Is it to be lit up constantly, so to speak, by the jagged lightning of God's special interventions and the aurora borealis of his signs and wonders rippling along the horizon? Or is the light that *normally* illumines the devout believer rather to be the wonder of knowing God, the certainty that he is the living God and the assurance that there is guidance, security and direction for the believing heart in the 'ordinary' reaches of life?

The obvious answer is the second. God made the world only once. That, as we have seen, was a 'wonder'. But equally wonderful, and much more frequently seen, is the daily wonder of the turning seasons, the fruitful crops, the order of nature. God only once rescued Israel from Egypt, and a second time brought her out of Babylon. Many Christians would wish to quote the twentieth-century return of Israel to its land as a third example. But the daily 'sign and portent' is his faithfulness to his ancient people when threatened by assimilation into surrounding paganisms (Isaiah 37:30–32). The modern equivalent is Christian people preserved in today's equally pagan and permissive society: sent *into* it but not *of* it.

Living in God's world

So the whole of life has meaning in its 'ordinary-ness'. The wonders of astronomy in its mathematical exactness and its mind-spinning immensities serve to underline the uniqueness and dignity of what it means to be a man created by God.

> When I look at thy heavens, the work of thy fingers,
>   the moon and the stars which thou hast established;
> what is man that thou art mindful of him...
> Yet thou hast made him little less than God,
>   and dost crown him with glory and honor.
> (Psalm 8:3–5)

No, the vastness of space is not a new thought, as C.S. Lewis used to delight to point out. Modern man often imagines that a large universe is a new concept making impossible a planet at the centre of God's purpose. In actual fact, 'More than seventeen hundred years ago Ptolemy taught that in relation to the distance of the fixed stars the whole earth must be regarded as a point with no magnitude. His astronomical system was universally accepted in the Dark and Middle Ages. The insignificance of Earth was as much a commonplace to King Alfred as it is to Professor Haldane.'[10]

The modern believer, fortified in his understanding of the immensity of the universe by new discoveries added to ancient theories, delights all the more in the glory of a divine love and purpose which has a place for him. It is God's universe. It is his Father's world.

If God commanded the sun to shine, he will also master

that cosmic sun of Satan caused by the unchained atom. If he knows that the earth with its plants and animals needs rain and therefore separates the waters under the firmament, he will also know the needs of the Queen of England, the orphan child in a children's home, and the aged pensioner. If a thousand years in his sight are but as yesterday, then in his eyes even my little cares will weigh no less than the immensities of Sirius. (Helmut Thielicke)[11]

Living in faith
God once heard and dramatically answered Elijah's cry for rain after drought (1 Kings 18:41–45). The New Testament draws our attention to it.

The prayer of a righteous man has great power in its effects. Elijah was a man of like nature with ourselves and he prayed fervently that it might not rain... Then he prayed again and the heaven gave rain (James 5:16–18).

The New Testament writer who points out the story, does so not to underline the need to live constantly in the miraculous, but to stress the need for *trust in God*. With equal emphasis he urges patient endurance; the virtue displayed so conspicuously by the prophets when their messages were derided, their warnings ignored and their characters impugned, and all they had to cling to was the certainty that God had spoken and was sovereignly at work (James 5:10–11).

In his great portrait gallery of faith's heroes, the New Testament writer to the Hebrews makes the same point. It is *faith expressed as faithfulness*, not faith vindicated in signs and wonders, that he exalts. Some indeed worked wonders. Abraham fathered a child in old age 'and him as good as dead'. Moses 'crossed the Red Sea as if on dry land'. Others 'stopped the mouths of lions... quenched raging fire… put foreign armies to flight.' There were even examples of life restored to the dead. Signs and wonders indeed! (*See* Hebrews 11)

But not for all was it so. 'Some were tortured.…others suffered mocking and scourging… were stoned, sawn in two, killed with the sword…' Was their faith any the less? Was God's intervention less evident or less sure in their case? Not at all. These, equally, are quoted as examples of faith. 'Well attested by their faith, [they] did not receive what was promised.' They received something better; a place in God's Kingdom when it was completed by the coming of the nations to Christ; 'God had foreseen something better …that apart from us they should not be made perfect' (*see* Hebrews 11).

A normal life?

In fact the 'normal' Old Testament life of faith and obedience is precisely that: normal! It features much more of divine sovereignty and divine providence, than divine intervention in astonishing ways. It even sounds a warning against being too easily impressed by astonishing signs.

> If a prophet arises among you, or a dreamer of dreams, and gives you a sign or a wonder, and the sign or wonder which he tells you comes to pass, and if he says, *'Let us go after other gods'* …you shall not listen… You shall walk after the Lord your God and fear him, and keep his commandments… (Deuteronomy 13:1–4)

Faithfulness to God *who has revealed himself in his Word* – that is the test.

This is why the book of Psalms speaks so powerfully to every generation. Here is the greatest 'experience-book' of the Old Testament. In it there is little that is not the familiar experience of the normal believer. The more dramatic acts of God referred to are usually in connection with the creation of the world and the rescue of Israel from Egypt. For the rest, God sometimes seems close and sometimes seems distant. The believer is often elated with faith and adoration, but equally often harassed, troubled, bewildered and full of doubts. Sometimes he gets near to despair. He prays constantly, but often his faith and patience are stretched by a long wait for an answer. The life of obedience sometimes pays splendid dividends, and sometimes leads only to scorn, rejection and apparent ill-fortune. The longest psalm of all puts it most clearly of all.

Here is a man who is constantly delighted by the fact that he has access to God's Word. He cannot find enough ways to describe the Bible. It is the *Law*, taught and revealed. It is the *testimony*, as if God were standing in court and bearing witness to it. It contains the *precepts*, instructions as detailed as those that a foreman gives to his work-force. Here are *statutes* as clear and detailed as local by-laws. Here are *commandments* backed by the powerful authority of God. There are *ordinances* to be found, like the first decisions of wise legal advisors. It is *the Word*, declared by God in offers and warnings. It is *the Promise* which contains the very words that God chose to use. *This* is the basis of Old Testament living. There is not (and need not be) a trace of the dry legalism, phariseeism and 'bibliolatry' which non-evangelicals darkly warn us against. It is God's Word, to be loved, searched, meditated and obeyed (*see* Psalm 119). [12]

The wonder of God's Book is the permanent sign of his authority and intervention: the daily wonder of a life lived within it is the sign that the world is most likely to notice.

Notes for chapter four

[1] The author has examined the area, as far as is possible in today's conditions. The place-names are still in use, and the whole topography and climate makes the event quite likely at intervals. Certainly it happened in 1906 and 1937.

[2] D. Guthrie, (ed.), *New Bible Commentary* (IVP, 1970), p.237.

[3]Conservative commentaries such as IVP *New Bible Commentary* regularly give this interpretation of the events.

[4]Elijah's ministry is described in 1 Kings 17–19.

[5]Elisha's story continues in 2 Kings 1–8.

[6]B.B. Warfield, *Counterfeit Miracles* (Banner of Truth, 1972). Originally delivered as a series of lectures in 1917-18.

[7]Quoted from an article on 'Miracles' by R. Martin-Achard in Von Allmen's *Vocabulary of the Bible* (English Translation, 1958).

[8]Alan Richardson, article on 'Miracles', in *The Word-Book of the Bible* (SCM, 1957), p.153.

[9]Martin-Achard, 'Miracles'.

[10]C.S. Lewis, *Miracles* (Fontana, 1960).

[11]Helmut Thielicke, *How the World Began* (James Clark & Co., 1964), p.19.

[12]Psalm 119. See Derek Kidner's analysis of the phrases used to describe the Word of God in *Psalms Tyndale Old Testament Commentary*, (IVP, 1975).

5

Declared to be the Son of God

'When our Lord came down to earth he drew heaven with him; the signs which accompanied his ministry were but the trailing clouds of glory which he brought from heaven which was his home.'[1]

In that one sentence the writer (the renowned Benjamin Warfield) hit a pre-emptive strike against every anticipated attack on the thesis of his whole book. For he went on to argue three propositions.

1. Such is the supernatural nature of the very coming of Christ that everything else supernatural is bound to spring from it.

2. Christ is totally unique in his ministry because he is totally unique in his person.

3. Only his immediate apostles could, by definition, display the same miraculous ministry.

Around the third proposition argument rages, and we shall have to return to it. But of the first two there can be no doubt among Christians who take the Bible seriously. The public ministry of Jesus of Nazareth was accompanied by an astonishing outburst of the supernatural. Here at least we do indeed find miracles on every page. From the gospel narratives we can at last say that the Bible (this part of it) is full of them.

In fact, thirty-five miracles are described individually. Twenty-three of them are concerned with physical healing. Three involve the ultimate in healing, namely raising from the dead after fatal illness. Nine could be called nature miracles, such as stilling a storm. Four involved creative power, like wine made from water. Four could be described as providential blessings, such as a remarkable catch of fish. One is an act of judgment in the withering of a fig tree which had proved fruitless and thereby carried a dark warning to the nation. The healings were applied to a wide variety of ailments including the dreaded leprosy, the widespread scourge of blindness, various types of paralysis, and several cases of exorcism.

But there was much more than this. It has been suggested with pardonable exaggeration that Jesus banished disease and death from Israel for three years. It is interesting to discover increasing evidence from recent excavations that the whole of the Galilee area, on account of its hot springs and mineral deposits, was one gigantic spa which attracted tens of thousands of people seeking healing. One of the Bible writers himself tells us with splendid hyperbole that the world could not contain the books that would be needed to record every great work that Jesus did. All of the gospel writers sprinkle their accounts with generalized references to a host of miracles not described in detail.

Ancient and modern

Matthew tells us Jesus 'went about...healing every disease and every infirmity among the people' (4:23). *Mark* tells how in Galilee, 'wherever he came, in villages, cities or country,' everyone who managed to touch his clothes was made well (6:56). *Luke,* a doctor himself, assures us that during one hour, and to underline a particular point, 'he cured many of diseases and plagues and evil spirits, and on many that were blind he bestowed sight' (7:21). *John*, who concentrates on the Jerusalem visits rather than the country ministry, contributes the surprising assertion that the Galileans came expectantly to Jesus in the first place only because of, 'all that he had done in Jerusalem' (4:5).

Modern writers will sometimes airily assure us that no-one now argues *from* the miraculous ministry of Jesus to the acceptance of the divine truth of his revelation. Arguments like the classic approach of William Paley are no longer convincing, since the average man no longer assumes that the gospel narratives are literally true and reliable. That, in fact, is largely the fault of critics who, purporting to be friends of the Bible, have imposed upon it treatment that would be laughed to scorn were it to be applied to the world's classics, and rejected with derision if it were applied to eye-witness accounts in a court of law.

In fact the case for the historicity of the gospel miracle stories is still a very strong one indeed, if the normal rules for examining historical documents are applied. All of the Gospels were written well within the lifetime of people involved in the events they purport to describe. When they were produced, it was in the interest of the great majority, both Jewish and Gentile, to crush them with facts that triumphantly prove their falsity. No-one seems to have done so. The writers sometimes insist on the most circumstantial details of time, place and person. Like the raising of Jairus' daughter for example (Mark 5). The ruler of the synagogue was the equivalent of a mayor and an Anglican rector rolled into one. It would have been very easy to rebut the story as a ridiculous fabrication about a well-known and respected family who indignantly denied the whole thing...unless it really happened!

Before long the Jewish authorities were very concerned to explain away the miracles of Jesus. They did so by attributing them to the black arts. It never seems to have occurred to them to say that they never happened. We are told that both the Jewish and the Gentile world of that time was awash with wonder stories, springing from a non-scientific attitude, worsened by one of those cycles of interest in the marvellous, through which human society seems to regularly move. This is so. The remarkable thing about the gospel narratives is their fundamental difference from such wonder stories. They are precisely nothing of the kind. The church a little later did misguidedly produce that sort of thing, or at any rate some of their less reputable fiction writers did so; a kind of second-century science fiction. A glance at it is sufficient to show the total difference. The boy Jesus makes model sparrows out of clay; he claps his hands, and they fly away. A school chum stumbles against him and injures him; Jesus puts a curse on him and he dies. The apostle Peter persuades a crowd to embrace Christianity by throwing a dead sardine into a swimming pool where it comes to life and circles merrily eating crumbs thrown to it. When the apostle Paul is beheaded, a jet of milk leaps from the severed head and splashes into the market square, which edifying sight persuades further converts. This kind of nonsense certainly never produced the gospel miracle stories from either a pagan, Jewish or Christian source.

Even the problems of the early church after the completion of the New Testament underline the same fact. They still believed in miracles, but were aware, it seems, of a falling-off both in quantity and quality. They produce hopeful examples, but rarely claim that they are really as impressive as the New Testament stories. How is it, then, that men who could not bring themselves to fake better wonders in their church had no compunction about forging them in their Bibles?

It became popular during the last century to attempt 'explanations' of Jesus' miracles in terms of the new sciences of psychology and sociology. Some of the healings were psychosomatic, it was suggested. Some owed their success to the power of Jesus' personality, some to a hypnotic-hysterical effect on the excited crowd, some to enthusiastic reports which circulated and grew bigger in the process. It may be that Jesus had unusual perceptiveness and discernment in his dealings with people... and so on. If such rationalizations had the purpose of reducing an unacceptable 'supernatural'element, then they really satisfied no-one but their propounders, for they quite missed the point. The undoubted fact is that healing was an integral part of the ministry of Christ. Whether every ailment healed was an organic disease beyond all other possible treatment; whether doctors now know more about the effect of mind-on-body than heretofore; all this is irrelevant. There is not the slightest evidence that Jesus said, or was supposed to have said, 'Anything you can do I can do better'. What is indisputable is that he left a memory (on friends and enemies alike) of a ministry to the whole person that involved care and compassion for people's physical, mental and spiritual need, the power to do something fundamental about it, and the assertion that in what was being done God was ushering in his kingdom, proclaiming his gospel, and drawing attention to his Son.

A more serious theological attempt to rationalize the miraculous was Bultmann's famous 'demythologizing' theory. Put simply, it went something like this. The word 'myth' properly used does not mean a fable, a nonsense or a fabrication. A myth is a reputable and legitimate literary form of words particularly appropriate for religious use. It must be assumed that absolute religious truth is 'beyond words', but myth is a method of reducing it to words. The words are in effect picture-stories. So, for example, the real truth is that Christ's gift of peace enables a man to live above the storms and disasters of life. This is put in myth form by telling of Jesus walking on the water to his disciples during a night storm on the lake. The words of Jesus can bring a sense of cleansing to the guilty conscience. This is mythologized by telling of him 'cleansing' a leper. Thus the task before a modern reader (how important it is to be *modern*; not true, or moral, or reasonable, but modern!) is to demythologize the stories of Jesus. Get behind the anecdotes to the real truth.

The language of truth

Theologians of this ilk were sharp enough to realize that the fundamental issue is the supernatural beginning and ending of the story. They did not hesitate to demythologize the virgin birth and the resurrection too. The 'real truth' behind the doctrine of the virgin birth thus becomes something like this: in Jesus all that can be expressed in human terms about God has been expressed. The Christmas story puts that into myth. Similarly with the resurrection. What really matters, we are assured, is that the disciples recovered from the terrible blow of the crucifixion of Jesus. They found that the power of his example, the memory of his personality, the truth of his teaching was still with them. It was effective. It survived his death. His 'spirit' was indeed with them. Something had come into this world with Jesus that would never disappear again. It was stronger than death. *Jesus* in fact (it could be said) was stronger than death. So the glorious conviction and experience began to be expressed in mythological forms; the stone which was rolled from the tomb, the people whose hearts were strangely warmed on the road home, the disciples who were recalled once more from fishing to catching men.

The approach has a certain attraction. There is a sense in which the 'meaning' is indeed more important than the detailed story. Does not every preacher treat it this way? What ladies' meeting has not been cheered by the promise that in the storms of life Jesus draws near? How many Sunday School children have heard the plea to give their little to God, and he will use it in wonderful ways, as Jesus shared the little boy's bread buns and sardines with five thousand people? What evangelist worthy of his salt has failed to draw encouraging lessons from the fact that the moral leper can be made clean, the morally paralysed given new strength, and the spiritually dumb set free to sing God's praises?

But of course that is not really demythologizing at all. It is *spiritualizing*. The Bible (and Jesus himself) encourages us to do it. The Christian sees a spiritual truth in *something which happened*. The approach of Bultmann (and all who have popularized him) simply denies that it happened at all. It cuts the jugular vein of the whole story of Jesus, by asserting that *it did not actually happen*. This is precisely the opposite of spiritualizing. That is seen clearly in the most fundamental story; the resurrection of Christ. What we are told in the Bible is precisely the opposite of the demythologizing version. The disciples did not tell resurrection stories because they became convinced that Jesus is stronger than death. They became convinced because he rose again and they met him.

> The Lord has risen indeed, and appeared to Simon!(Luke 24:34)
> To them he presented himself alive after his passion by many proofs. (Acts 1:3)
> He appeared to more than five hundred brethren...most of whom are still alive. (1 Corinthians 15:6)

That is the language of the disciples. Their conviction did not create a story; rather their experience created a conviction.

The same is true of the whole gospel narrative. Demythologizing reverses the entire thrust of it and makes a nonsense of it. We know that God loves the untouchable, precisely because Jesus touched the leper. We know that

73

God comes to us in our weakness and humanity, precisely because he was incarnate in the baby of Bethlehem.

> …this will be a sign for you: you will find a babe wrapped in swaddling cloths and lying in a manger (Luke 2:12).

Once accept that God was uniquely, supernaturally, unimaginably at work in Christ for our salvation; once accept that he was born the way we are told he was and conquered death the way we are told he did; once open your life to the breath-taking possibility of the direct intervention of God…and the lesser wonders of multiplied loaves and lame men leaping will seem inevitable, even natural. But once reject this beginning and ending, and the stories in between are of no significance anyway, for they do not tell us anything about God at all. They do not even tell us anything about the historical figure of Jesus. They do not tell us anything that actually happened. A 'myth', in short, is not a serious option at all. There is not the remotest evidence that any of the truly mythological figures of literature and religion ever lived. C.S. Lewis, Professor of Literature and therefore possibly knowledgeable on such subjects, comments:

> I have been reading poems, romances, vision literature, myths all my life, I know what they are like. I know none of them is like this…. The reader who doesn't see this simply has not learned to read.[2]

Jesus in action

So then the miracles of Jesus must be taken seriously. Let us now try to do so. We need to, for there are some important questions to explore. If they really happened then, are we to expect them really to happen now? Alternatively, if they really happened then to someone in every way totally unique, does that still leave us not expecting them to happen now? And whatever are we to make of these memorable and haunting words of Jesus:

> He who believes in me will also do the works that I do; and greater works than these will he do (John 14:12).

The works that *he* does? *Greater* works?

How are we to understand these remarkable works of Christ? What was their nature, their purpose, their significance? The gospel narratives give us plenty of clues. They are found in the words which the writers employ, which include the exact Greek equivalents of the Hebrew synonyms for 'miracle' which we have already examined (*see* pages 56–57). They are more than hinted at in the vivid details of some of the stories. Sometimes they are explained and applied in so many words by Jesus himself. Perhaps most significant of all are the different ways in which the four gospel writers handle their material and group their stories.

Love in action

Some of the healings are said to originate in the simplest and most affecting motive; human sympathy. We see Jesus 'moved with compassion' at the sight of suffering. He is indignant at the sight of a man's infirmity being exploited by others (Mark 3:5). He is touched by the plight of a weeping widow who has now lost her son (Luke 7:11–12). He sobs himself as he sees the sorrow at the tomb of a friend (John 11:28–39). There is much significance in the manner in which he touches sufferers (even embraces them, as one word suggests.) The effect of that alone on an outcast leper must have been enormous (Matthew 8:1–3). Here is human compassion touched with divine power.

75

On to the offensive

Some miracles bear all the marks of conflict. Jesus is invading enemy-occupied territory, so to speak. There is an element of deliverance-from-bondage, and the enemy is named. A crippled woman has been 'bound by Satan', and is rescued. Against the crude charge of employing the black arts, he points out that it is precisely the devil's kingdom that is being injured by his actions. Everywhere he goes, he does good, heals the sick, and rescues those who are afflicted by the devil (Acts 10:38 gives Peter's summary of Jesus' ministry). His ejection of demons from their victims is of course the most vivid expression of this. Perhaps it is significant that in these cases he is never described as touching the victim; rather he sharply commands the enemy. His enigmatic comment on all this is, 'I saw Satan fall like lightning from heaven' (Luke 10:18).

Divine authentication

Sometimes Jesus appealed to his actions as authentication by God of his claims and his words. Seeing the shocked expressions of those who heard him announce forgiveness of sin, he went on to heal the paralysis of the penitent sinner, 'that you might know that the Son of man has authority on earth to forgive sins' (Mark 2:1–12). On one occasion he makes the rather unusual plea that if the power of his words, charged with truth, is not enough to convince his hearers, then they should believe because of the works that he does (John 10:36–38). However, this is very far from the claim that marvellous deeds of themselves can convince people of truth, as we shall see. It is rather that those who already recognize and rejoice in the truth from God will see confirmation for their faith in the works that accompany the words.

'The works which the Father has granted me to accomplish, these very works which I am doing, bear me witness that the Father has sent me… His voice you have never heard, his form you have never seen; and you do not have his word abiding in you, for you do not believe him whom he has sent' (John 5:36–38). This is a typical elliptical argument from John's Gospel. The Son of God brings truth to those who welcome it. God confirms that truth by 'works' which are not only powerful but charged with truth. But for those who are determined to live in error, neither the words not the works will be found convincing. This thought leads directly to the next theme.

The appeal to faith

On very many occasions, Jesus himself links faith with miracles. When desperate men interrupt a house-meeting by breaking through the roof to attract his attention to their paralysed friend, 'seeing their faith' he answers their plea. When an embarrassed woman with a haemorrhage shyly touches the hem of his robe and finds healing, he insists on calling her back and underlining that it is her faith not her touch that has effected the cure. He commends in the highest terms a Roman officer who believes that an illness can be dealt with by a word of command from Jesus (Matthew 8:8). He actively encourages faith's activity in prayer, in dangerous circumstances, in emulating him by serving others (Mark 4:35–41; Luke 11:9).

It should be emphasized that this is not *faith healing* as it is often understood and practised today. It may very well be true that faith has remarkable power in itself over the mind and the body. That is illustrated not only in hysterical and psychosomatic illnesses but in the whole effect that expectation, optimism, excitement and positive thinking have on the will and the healing processes. In such cases the *object* of the faith is almost irrelevant, as long as the expectation is activated. It may be the shrine of Mary at Lourdes, the teaching of Mary Baker Eddy, or the exhortation of an itinerant pseudo-pentecostal healer to touch the screen of the television set; something will sometimes happen and faith-healing is a fairly accurate phrase to describe it. The faith which Jesus invited and urged was something quite different. It was faith in his unique person, his mission, his message. It was surrender to his purposes, whether they be to heal an infirmity, to change a life-style, or to lead on a path that would end in martyrdom.

Consequently, Jesus' healing-miracles very rarely carry the message, 'Believe because you see'. Rather they are illustrations of the power of faith when it is rightly focused. Jesus, by performing these compassionate acts, invites, stimulates and calls into action, faith in the love and power of God revealed in the Messiah whom he has sent. Jesus, not his wonderful works, is the object of belief; his works are simply pointers to faith.

Clues to identity
Sometimes by cautious hint, sometimes by mere allusion which could easily be missed, and sometimes by direct statement, Jesus without doubt announced himself as God's promised Messiah and presented his 'works' as evidence. 'Is the Christ to come from Galilee?' the amazed crowd often asked, and he left them to work it out, without comment (*e.g.* John 7:41). By the time he entered Jerusalem for the last time, many had come to their own conclusions, and quoted his miracles in support (Matthew 21:1–10). John the Baptist during an understandable spell of depression and disappointment, asked outright: 'Are you he who is to come, or shall we look for another?' Jesus told those who conveyed the question to go back and tell John what they have seen

the blind receive their sight and the lame walk, lepers are cleansed and the deaf hear, and the dead are raised up, and the poor have good news preached to them (Matthew 11:2–6).

What is Jesus saying? Not merely that the working of wonders proves him to be the promised Messiah. It is the nature of those wonders that tells the story and gives the meaning. They are healings. They speak of rescue and deliverance from blindness, lameness, uncleanness and inability to hear... even from death. They are full of rich spiritual promise and symbolism. They are gospel announcements. Moreover, they fulfil the explicit promises of the Old Testament with regard to the coming Messiah.

> Then the eyes of the blind shall be opened,
>   and the ears of the deaf unstopped;
> then shall the lame man leap like a hart,
>   and the tongue of the dumb sing for joy.
> (Isaiah 35:5–6)

Charles Wesley caught up the same evangelical significance in one of his hymns ('O for a thousand tongues,') and applied it to the revival scenes in eighteenth-century England when the poor indeed had the gospel of Christ preached to them for the first time in their generation:-

> Hear Him, ye deaf; his praise, ye dumb,
>   Your loosened tongues employ;
> Ye blind, behold your Saviour come;
>   And leap, ye lame, for joy!

The same point was made when Jesus first returned to his home town of Nazareth and preached in the synagogue. Deliberately (and to them offensively) recalling miracles of Elijah and Elisha, with all their prophetic and Messianic overtones, he quotes the lovely words which Isaiah puts into the mouth of the coming Christ (as they well understood)

'The Spirit of the Lord is upon me,
because he has anointed me to
    preach good news to the poor.
He has sent me to proclaim release to the captives
and recovery of sight to the blind,
to set at liberty those who are oppressed,
to proclaim the acceptable year of the Lord.'
(Luke 4:18–30, quoted from Isaiah 61:1–2)

At one of the great climax-points in the story, Jesus deliberately provokes his followers to get beyond the popular opinions prevalent at that time and make up their minds as to who he really is. 'You are the Christ, the Son of God', is Peter's sturdy reply. Jesus accepts the title and praises Peter's answer which he asserts was beyond human shrewdness but was revealed by God. On this truth, his church would be built (Matthew 16:13–17). He is the Messiah. They have read the signs aright.

Wonderful works

This word, usually simply translated *wonders* (as in its Old Testament equivalent, *see* page 56) emphasizes the effect produced upon the onlookers. Thus the writers often describe this with evident eye-witness memory. When a paralytic walked, 'they were amazed and glorified God, saying "We never saw anything like this."' When a storm was stilled at his command, 'they were filled with awe and said to one another, "Who then is this that even wind and sea obey him?"' This is the most superficial word used to describe the miracles and it is significant that it is never used alone in the New Testament, but is always associated with the other word 'sign' but once again we have the familiar phrase, 'signs and wonders'. 'The miracles of Jesus are not mere wonders intended to strike the imagination. There is a close relation between these marvellous events and the person of him who does them. They are visible emblems of what he is and what he came to do.' So said Origen in the third century.

Signs that speak to the understanding

So we come to the most important synonym for the supernatural act in the ministry of Jesus, as in the Old Testament. A *sign* acts as a summons. 'Open your eyes to the spiritual appeal that is about to be addressed to you.'; this is what a sign commands. This is precisely how the apostles understood the miracles as we shall see in a later chapter. This is a descriptive word most commonly used in the gospel narratives, though unfortunately in the Authorized Version it is often translated as the vaguer word *miracle*. By presenting itself as a sign, the deed draws attention not to itself but to the one who performs it. A sign promotes a question, 'What does this mean?', rather than the exclamation, 'How marvellous!'

This is why Jesus rebuked the crowd after the feeding of the five thousand as described in John 6:26 (in a manner obscured by the translation in the Authorized Version). He did not say, 'Ye seek me, not because ye saw the miracles'. That was precisely why they did seek him; they wanted a repeat performance of such a splendid welfare opportunity as a few pieces of bread and fish multiplied to feed thousands. What he said to them was, 'You seek me, not because you saw *signs,* but because you ate your fill of the loaves.'

'You saw the loaves multiply, but you did not see its significance. It was, to you, a wonder but not a sign.' That is a fair paraphrase of Jesus' rebuke. 'You came with no higher thought than that of another meal. Yet I can give you eternal food for your inner being; that is the real significance of the sign. I am the bread of life... believe in me.'

81

This perfectly expresses the meaning of a sign. It also underlines its limitations. For much now depends on the attitude of the onlooker. Does he merely watch and gasp? Does he ponder and believe? Does he see the significance but reject it? This underlines a remarkable fact. Jesus often played down the value of signs, and even refused to supply them. When Jesus scandalized the Jewish authorities by storming into the temple and ejecting the money-changers, they asked him, 'What sign have you to show us for doing this?' (John 2:18) Jesus' only reply was so enigmatic that they never understood it and even the disciples themselves made little of it until after the crucifixion and resurrection.

When much later some of the Scribes and Pharisees asked, 'Teacher, we wish to see a sign from you' (Matthew 12:38–39) he answered them abruptly with a refusal to give any sign to an adulterous generation seeking for signs. Then another mysterious reference to his coming death and resurrection follows in chapter 16, this time linking it with 'the sign of the prophet Jonah'. Once again he totally disappointed them when on being asked for 'a sign from heaven', he simply pointed out ironically to them that although they could make fairly accurate weather forecasts from signs in the sky, they seemed incapable of interpreting 'the signs of the times' and once again called them an evil and adulterous generation seeking for a sign when none would be given but the sign of Jonah (Matthew 16:4).

Immediately after this he sternly warned the disciples themselves of the danger of falling under the corrupting influence of the Pharisees and Sadducees whose whole approach to signs made it impossible for them to see any significance in them. The disciples themselves were in danger of having the same attitude and failing, for example, to see the real significance of the feeding of the five thousand. 'How is it that you fail to perceive…?' asks Jesus sadly. 'O men of little faith,…Do you not yet perceive? Do you not remember the five loaves?' (Matthew 16:8–9)

Most striking of all when Jesus stood on trial before the puppet-king Herod, we find that his 'judge' was 'very glad, for he had long desired to see him, because he had heard about him, and he was hoping to see some sign done by him' (Luke 23:6–12). Jesus totally declined to oblige with any marvellous work, any significant action or even any word. Though Herod had used the word sign, this was not what he wanted at all. He desired to have his curiosity satisfied and his appetite whetted by some marvel that would set him gaping, and give him something to relate to his friends at some future dinner. To such a person Jesus has nothing to say. To such a mind a sign has no significance and therefore ceases to be truly a sign.

But for those who have eyes to see, signs are illuminating and revealing. Most of all they reveal who Jesus is. So his power over the demons is a sign that Satan's kingdom is being cast down and the strong man bound (Luke 11:17–23). His healing of physical disease (almost universally believed to be directly connected with specific sin) is the sign of his power to forgive sins (Mark 2:1–12). His influence over the forces of nature is a sign of his essential unity with the God of the Old Testament, of whom it is written, 'He made the storm be still, and the waves of the sea were hushed' (Psalm 107:29). Equally, as we have seen, the feeding miracles show Christ to be the giver of the bread of life. The bringing of a lame man back to a new life of normal activity becomes a sign of the ability of the Saviour to bring new spiritual life to the believer. The raising of a friend from death is a sign that Jesus is 'the resurrection and the life'.

Acts of power

This word *dynamis* (with its obvious English connotations) is the third great descriptive word in the gospel story. 'He began to upbraid the cities where most of his *mighty works* were done' (my italics) we read in Matthew 11:20–24. It is the equivalent of the Hebrew word used to describe God's mighty deeds in rescuing Israel from Egypt, ordering the created universe, and destroying the enemies of the godly. A frightened dictator whose conscience is troubling him worries about 'these powers at work in him' (*i.e.* John the Baptist, Matthew 14:1–2). The emphasis lies in the moral power rather than in the question of whether or not the works are 'miraculous'. So in the above references, the Galilean cities should have been moved to repentance by them, and Herod should have learned the moral lesson. So, significantly, the same word is used by Paul to describe the power at work in the gospel revealing God's righteousness and making bad men good (Romans 1:16–17; Ephesians 1:21).

God at work

One more word is a favourite of John's. He shows us Jesus performing what are simply called *works (erga)*. We shall return to this. Suffice to say now, that miracles which shook Jerusalem and had the whole city in an uproar of debate (John 5:36; 10:25) are described by a surprisingly homely word which can equally well describe a job undertaken, a Christian act of charity, or a serious effort to keep the law (Acts 13:2; Romans 9:32; James 1:25–27). It is as if the gospel writer is saying, 'this is what Jesus did because he was that kind of person'. He acted according to his nature. His nature was wonderful, compassionate and revelatory of God's truth, and so accordingly were his works. The great miracle was the incarnation; all else follows naturally. It is no wonder that he whose name is Wonderful (Isaiah 9:6) did works of wonder; the greater wonder would be if he had never done them!

Only then, or still today?

We can now begin to approach some assessment of Christ's miracles. To what extent were they unique to him? What relationship do they bear to activities today which draw attention to the supernatural? First we need to establish some negatives.

They were not examples of 'spiritual' healing. The phrase today is used loosely to describe healings which are unrelated to orthodox or unorthodox medicine, and which appeal in various degrees to 'the spiritual world'. This includes Spiritualism, the use of 'guides' and 'mediums', the outright invoking of magic, and some forms of yoga and meditation in which the names of Eastern deities are chanted or held in the mind. To all such, the biblical command is clear. They are forbidden by God, and involve a rebellion against his will and his word (Deuteronomy 18:9–22; Isaiah 8:16–20). They are not all to be dismissed as fakes, but they are all to be avoided as forbidden territory. It is possible for people to achieve impressive results by occult methods and even to claim Jesus as some kind of authority in them, and yet for the Son of God totally to disown them in the day of judgment as 'evildoers' (Matthew 7:15–23).

It might seem that such a warning is unnecessary for Christians. But an attitude of 'wonders at any cost' can lead the believer into dubious territory, to say the least. There are, of course, Christians of total integrity involved in various 'deliverance and healing ministries'. Sadly, there are others whose source of inspiration seems more dubious and who hover half-way between orthodox Christianity and the occult. Some claim to be mainline Christians and some are leaders of semi-Christian fringe cults. I recall one with a 'gospel and healing ministry' whose whole base was the remembrance and repetition of occult-type experiences of being levitated, hearing voices, seeing visions, having marvellous experiences... all 'from the Lord' of course, but bearing no relation to anything in the ministry of Jesus. A very occasional Bible quotation cropped up, but he had no time for doctrine or theology. Dismissing anyone who tried to apply the Scriptures to his ministry, he replied, 'They quote doctrine but I do miracles'. In essence, this man had little more relationship to the recorded ministry of Jesus than another, an avowed leader of a church-hating cult who rejected every Scripture I quoted with assertion, 'Look, all you've got is the Bible, but Christ himself often visits me'. The 'Christ' who often 'visited' him was then quoted in support of lying, immorality, and blatantly false doctrine.

They were not attention-drawing crusades. One cannot doubt the sincerity and indeed the Christianity of many who engage in healing-crusades. I simply make the point that *this is not what Jesus did*. He did not advertise healings, as a method of gathering crowds. He did not publish promises in advance and invite the public to come and watch the blind receiving sight and the lame walking. Certainly his healings very often drew crowds, but he frequently discouraged those who benefited, from creating further excitement (Mark 3:7–12; 5: 35–43).

It is sometimes argued that a more overtly miracle-working church would draw in people, especially the working-classes whom she often fails to reach. If little Jimmy in some 'Coronation Street' were to be marvellously healed, *that* would get them into St Judes-on-the-corner in a way that mere pulpit-preaching can never do. It is an attractive thought, but there seems little evidence. The writer has seen a number of cases of very impressive healings in answer to prayer during the pastorates of three successive churches. Doctors have acknowledged them to be hard or impossible to explain. They had little effect on the evangelism of those churches, and I can think of no conversion directly resulting from them.

During the same period and in the same churches there have been several hundred conversions as a result of public preaching and private witnessing. This should not surprise us. Few of the miracles of Jesus led to conversion. Whole towns declined to 'repent' when confronted with them. Jesus said quite specifically that if people are not convinced by 'Moses and the prophets' (*i.e.* the Bible) then they will not be convinced even by someone returning from the dead (Luke 16:27–31). What could be more clear?

There can be no doubt that in some areas of the world (perhaps especially parts of South America and Asia) the powerful spread of Scripture and gospel by means of dedicated witnesses is being accompanied by 'signs and wonders'. Where that is so, they fulfil their great biblical purpose, which is to 'confirm' the word of truth, not to create it or replace it (Acts 2:42–43).

They were not examples of faith-healing. This has been suggested already. Certainly Jesus emphasized the importance of faith. But this was faith in himself, his person and his mission. 'Faith' as an attitude of mind can sometimes work wonders, but the gospel records tell us, not of faith working wonders, rather of Christ working wonders. The assertion sometimes made that faith must produce the desired result, cannot seriously be drawn from Christ's ministry. He certainly advocates faith but what he says must by balanced by what he says elsewhere about the will of God, about the prior importance of the soul's salvation, about the importance of obedience and submission, and about the inevitability of suffering, conflict and persecution for the true disciple.

The faith which Jesus demands of those who come to him to be cured is not, of course, faith in the modern sense of 'faith-healing' – such a notion is utterly foreign to the Gospel atmosphere – but a believing relation and attitude towards his own person.[3]

The mechanical and inevitable equation of faith with desired result has two consequences. It commits the propagator (in his 'healing ministry') to a cruel and irresponsible get-out when nothing happens. Quite often something does happen, for such a person often proclaims Christ with earnestness and conviction. But he himself never faces hard facts (the 'failure' in his own terms of a great proportion of his healings). He never comes to a more sound and balanced equation; for the 'cop-out' is always there. They didn't have enough faith! His position is impregnable. It can resist every attack of common-sense, factual observation and theological questioning.

More serious still is the harm done to the sufferer who was not healed. It is his fault. Either he did not believe earnestly enough, or he is locked in some disobedience. He cannot identify it if he is over-confident, or he identifies it only too readily in a dozen places if he is over-sensitive. Every pastor of any sizeable community had to comfort and guide the sad victims.

They were not examples of human faith at work. A subtle variation of the previous idea is sometimes found. The miracle-minister presents his own ministry as an example of what we can all do for others if we only believe. It is possible to preach on some of the great miracle-stories as examples of faith-in-action. Mark's Gospel undoubtedly underlines something like this, as we shall see presently. The reasoning then goes as follows. See what Jesus did by faith. If you have faith, you can do the same.

I recall being surprised and taken aback by a question in my ordination exam. 'Describe Jesus as a man of faith.' I found it difficult, because although Jesus was undoubtedly a man of faith (and courage, and prayer, and every other virtue!) he was more than that. He was the Son of God! His mighty works illustrated not only faith, but his unique and invariable obedience to the Father, and his unique offices as Saviour, Redeemer, Messiah, King and Lord. Demons fled from him, not because he believed they would, but because they knew him to be the Son of God. Sickness melted away at his touch not because he believed it would but because he always, only, ever acted as the Father commanded him to act. We must beware of the unintended arrogance which edges us near to saying, 'I am another Jesus'.

I say this because I have heard at least one respected Christian itinerant adopt this reasoning with a large and excited congregation, and I have seen some of the fanaticism that it has led to.

They were not examples of healing-by-counselling. As the Christian Church begins to take more seriously its ministry to the 'whole man' there are increasing numbers of healing centres and counselling centres springing up. Some are an integral part of established denominations (like the Church of England or the Baptist Union). Others are independent and self-supporting. They are very often centres of sanity, compassion and dedicated service. Sometimes the workers are trained in medical skills, counselling techniques, psychiatry or social sciences. Sometimes they depend entirely on 'spiritual' principles such as community living, confession and sharing of forgiveness, prayer, healing of traumatic memories, learning to be rid of bitterness and self-centredness, *etc.*

The theological approach varies a great deal, and so does the methodology. Some have a pronounced sacramental flavour, some depend on prolonged counselling, and some exercise a ministry of the laying-on of hands with or without a charismatic emphasis. It would be difficult to speak too highly of them. Most Christian leaders see examples of their effectiveness. I certainly do.

It is not any denigration to say that this is not quite the same thing as the miraculous ministry of Jesus. It undoubtedly reflects the spirit of his ministry. Its motivation is the imitation of Christ. Its success is due to the power and relevance of the gospel at every level of human life. It is simply not the same thing, and few would say that it was. It is Christ's ministry today, through his disciples, not Christ's ministry in first-century Galilee in person. *This* says 'God's love and power is at work whenever his selfless servants go in his name'. *That* said, 'The Kingdom of God is breaking upon you. The Son has come. Behold him, whilst the light is still shining.'

They were not examples of the gifts of the Spirit in the Church. That should be obvious. The Spirit had not come. The church was not formed. Without doubt, the New Testament speaks of the working of charismatic gifts within the limbs of the body, Christ being the head. But that is not an explanation of the Galilee and Jerusalem ministry of Jesus. The body of Christ *then* was the literal body which God had prepared for him (Hebrews 10:5) and in which he delighted his Father in deeds perfect and infallible. The body of Christ *now* is the spiritual body of the church, through which he expresses his will (imperfectly because we are imperfect, fallibly because we are fallible).

This is important. We have seen that we must not regard Jesus simply as a man of faith and therefore imagine that we can be the same. Equally we must not regard the unique incarnation of the Son of God in Jesus as if it were totally paralleled by the ongoing activity of Jesus in his body the church, and imagine that the situation is the same.

In a moving and persuasive exposition, Tom Smail outlines how far we can go, seeing in Jesus the pattern for the

Spirit-filled believer. Like him we may be anointed by the Holy Spirit. Like him we will subsequently find ourselves confronting a suffering Satan-dominated society. Like him we can act in the confidence of a loving and powerful Father. As for him, so for us, there will be death and resurrection (though of a very different kind). Like him we should expect power and deeds to accompany words and teaching, so that people are not only informed but changed. Very rightly he suggests that this pattern may well provide a model for dynamic renewal today that is more balanced and biblical than a second-blessing type of approach. But this has its limits. Jesus was not a Spirit-filled believer; he was the Son of God declared with power! I am not Jesus, and never can be! Smail refers movingly to an incident basic to the rise of 'Irvingism' in the nineteenth century, as a kind of precursor of Pentecostalism and Charismatic Renewal.

> (Mary Campbell) straightway argued, if Jesus as a man in my nature thus spake and thus performed mighty works by the Holy Ghost, which he even promiseth me, then I ought in the same nature, by the same Spirit to do likewise the works which he did and greater works than these. Having thus argued with herself Mary Campbell first began to speak in tongues and then rose from her bed healed.[4]

But the logic can be taken only so far. I may follow Jesus in the pattern of a man filled with the Spirit, but I cannot even begin to imitate him as the only begotten Son of God. I can apply the great lessons of faith and obedience as he did in subjection to the Father as truly man, but I cannot remotely approach his pathway as the promised Christ.

Nor could Mary Campbell. Earnest and sincere, prayerful and dedicated as she was, she shared human fallibility, frailty and at times even folly. The movement which her experience galvanized drifted into serious errors of faith and practice. The biblical preaching of its leader Edward Irving was increasingly overshadowed by excited scenes of emotion and a hunger for the spectacular. Scripture exposition was interrupted by 'prophecies' sometimes of dubious value. Some leaders admitted that in their anxiety to see signs and wonders they had induced them. Mary Campbell herself gravely misunderstood her 'tongues' as a supernatural endowment of Turkish and Chinese designed to equip her to preach to foreigners without learning the language. Actual missionary work abroad speedily disillusioned her, and she dropped the practice altogether. This all makes sad reading, and should be regarded with charity and sympathy. These were dedicated Christians whose zeal and commitment should shame many of us, but in some areas of life they were mistaken and they failed in obedience. That puts them (like all of us) in a different category from Jesus Christ. He was never mistaken. He never failed in obedience. He was more than a Spirit-filled man. He was more than 'a man in my nature (who) performed mighty works by the Holy Ghost'. He was the unique and perfect Son of God.

Whatever God has promised by his Holy Spirit (and we shall see that he has promised a great deal), he has not promised an infallibility and a perfection that bring us into the everyday exercise of the ministry and mighty works of Jesus. The exercise of God's gifts within the church which is Christ's body is a wonderful thing, but it is not that. We must now return to the gospel accounts and see what they do teach us about Christ's work in that day and in this.

Notes for chapter five

[1]B.B. Warfield, *Counterfeit Miracles* (Banner of Truth, 1972), opening sentence.
[2]C.S. Lewis, *Miracles* (Fontana, 1960), chapter 14.
[3]Alan Richardson, *The Word-Book of the Bible* (SCM, 1957), p. 153.
[4]T. Smail, *Reflected Glory* (Hodder, 1975), p.74.

6

Many pictures, one Lord

Jesus Christ is alive today. Men and women become Christians by engaging in a living encounter with him which brings them forgiveness of sin, a new heart and a personal relationship with God. Nothing less than this is the Christian gospel.

As I write this I have in the last few days talked to several people who have told me of meeting Christ and finding new life in him. They include a middle-aged widow, a young business man, a university student, a young married couple, a doctor's receptionist and a factory worker. Their stories differ in detail but are alike in essentials. They have been 'born anew to a living hope through the resurrection of Jesus Christ from the dead' (1Peter 1:3). What has happened is considerably more than being impressed by the story of Christ, captivated by the character of Christ or influenced by the teaching of Christ. They have met Christ. He has given them life.

Clearly this has enormous implications for life-style, morality, religious practice, attitudes and character. These are beyond the scope of this enquiry. What we must try to explore here is what the *miraculous* ministry of Christ implies for today's experience. Does he still work that way today?

Here is a simple and fairly common example. An itinerant preacher with a healing and evangelistic ministry prefaces his preaching with a 'testimony'. Indeed, his whole address may well be his testimony, liberally sprinkled with Scripture texts. It goes something like this. He was brought up as a boy in 'church'. Perhaps he sang in the choir. Then came the teenage years and he drifted away, seeing no reality in it. Later a time of crisis caused him to think again about spiritual issues. He vaguely remembered hearing somewhere in the Bible, 'Jesus Christ is the same yesterday, today and for ever'(Hebrews 13:8).

He went back to church, but they didn't seem to think so. They talked religion, but not Jesus. He tried another church, and there they did talk about Jesus. Indeed, they spoke of trusting him and knowing him. But when he asked for evidence that Jesus is the same today as ever, they had none. Jesus used to heal the lame, but now you go to an osteopath. Jesus used to make the blind see, but now you ask God's help to make you patient and brave your blindness. Disappointed, he tried another church.

This time it was different! They prayed with a man in a wheelchair, and he tottered down the aisle without it. They laid hands on a lady with arthritis and the pain left her. The seeker felt that at last he had found. Here was a living proof of the living Christ, doing what he had done in Galilee long ago. Jesus Christ was, indeed, the same yesterday, today and for ever. He surrendered his faith and obedience. A sense of peace came to him. Soon he found to his amazement that he, too, could lay hands on people and see remarkable things happening.

That, I think, is a not unfair summary of quite a common type of testimony. Shortly before writing this I heard one very like it, and on that particular occasion could find no fault with the reverent, restrained and balanced way in which the 'ministry' was afterwards offered. But the testimony itself still raised questions in one listener's mind at least. Two questions specifically: is this what the Bible means by saying that Jesus is 'the same' today? And is this the gospel as we find it presented in the New Testament? Is the gospel the announcement that Jesus is visibly at work today meeting people's physical needs, and that evidence of this should bring us to a commitment to him? Or is the gospel about a spiritual encounter with Christ which brings us to changed attitudes and an act of faith in his 'naked word', so to speak. Where do we fit into those words of Jesus when he said to hesitating Thomas, 'Have you believed because you have seen me? Blessed are those who have not seen and yet believe...' (John 20:26–29).

Perhaps we can pose the question another way. The New Testament presents us with a picture of Jesus Christ. It asserts that he is still at work in every generation in which its pages are read. Then what does it lead us to expect when we put our faith in that Christ? What features of the story of Jesus in Jerusalem and Galilee are we encouraged to expect to see in our own lives as we believe?

Obviously we begin with the gospel records of Matthew, Mark and John. (Luke's account will be examined together with Acts in the following chapter). There are evident differences, but even more obvious likenesses. Quite clearly, each writer is being selective in what he records. Equally clearly the selected stories have a shape and a purpose. The writers have a message to pass on.

Mark – and the man for others

Many scholars believe that Mark was the first of the gospel writers and that Matthew and Luke draw a great deal of their material from him. There is a very ancient and persuasive tradition that Mark's Gospel is, to all intents and purposes, Peter's Gospel since the apostle virtually dictated to his young nephew Mark his memoirs of exciting days in Galilee with Jesus.[1] Tradition claims that Peter was by that time resident in Rome and there is a great deal to be said for regarding this very manly and energetic account as being particularly shaped to appeal to the Roman character.

The first question that a Roman would be likely to ask when being told of Jesus of Nazareth would be simply, 'What did he *do*?' This Gospel certainly answers that question with gusto. The word *euthus* – immediately – constantly appears in this exciting and almost breathless narrative. The story rushes us from one active and colourful incident to another. The repeated use of the word *immediately* seems to make the writer say to us, 'And the very next thing that happened was....' and away we go on the next adventure.

Many devout Bible readers have delighted to point out the close similarity there is between Peter's simple explanation of the gospel to *Roman* listeners in the household of the centurion Cornelius (Acts 10:34–43) and the outline of the Gospel according to Mark. John the Baptist appears preparing the way for Jesus. Jesus is anointed with the Holy Spirit and launches out on his great ministry of healing, exorcism and deliverance. He moves on from the countryside to the great city of Jerusalem. There he is arrested, condemned and crucified. On the third day God raises him from the dead and he is seen, not by all and sundry but by a few chosen witnesses. To them he gives a special command that they should go out and preach the good news to all who are eager to receive the forgiveness of sins through his name. That is the skeleton of Peter's 'sermon' and that is precisely the order of events and the emphasis of Mark's Gospel.

At least twenty-one of the recorded miracles of Jesus appear in detail in this particular Gospel; by far the most frequent. They are told with a vivid sense of being eyewitness accounts. It is not really surprising that a modern actor can fill a theatre by simply declaiming with appropriate inflexion and gestures the whole narrative from

Mark in the Authorized Version. But this is no mere list of wonder stories. The healings, for example, are not simply that but are illustrations of the power of faith which Jesus invites, stimulates and calls into action among those whom he encounters. The purpose is not to draw attention to healings. The purpose is not even to persuade the reader to believe that similar healings could happen to him. The purpose quite clearly is to point a finger of attention and instruction to the wondrous person who grants those healings.

Words and deeds of authority

Exousia (authority) is the key word in the first cycle of stories which runs through the first to the third chapters. Jesus is authorized by the voice from heaven and the descending Spirit in the form of a dove. He begins to preach with the tremendous claim that the Kingdom of God is at hand. He meets Simon and Andrew and James and John and bluntly commands them to leave their occupation and follow him; no explanation, no argument, just follow (Mark 1:9–20).

He preaches in the local synagogue and people are astonished at the authority which is expressed in his teaching. He is interrupted by a demon-possessed man whose tormentor is prepared to acknowledge that he is the holy one of God. Jesus speaks with powerful authority and commands the spirit to leave the victim. Light and power, words and deeds seem to stream from this remarkable man as he confronts one situation after another – sickness, despair and sorrow. In private house and in crowded street Jesus dismisses sickness as if it were a cowed and defeated enemy which must flee at his presence (Mark 1:21–45).

The pace quickens and the authority becomes even more evident. Jesus shocks the religious-minded by announcing that a man's sin is forgiven; an announcement which they rightly understand can come only with the authority of the

God against whom alone sin by definition is committed. 'But that you may know that the Son of man has authority on earth to forgive sins... I say to you rise, take up your pallet and go home' and the man does so. Jesus hurries on to interview a despised and loathed tax collector who has compromised his race and his religion by working for the occupying power. A simple word of command causes the man to leave his occupation and to become a follower of Jesus. It is difficult to say what is more astonishing – the fact that he went or the fact that Jesus invited him.

The point is underlined in two incidents that immediately follow when religious leaders criticize Jesus for not being at all particular about the company that he keeps. He quotes in justification the Old Testament picture of God as the divine physician with the obvious implication that it is those, who are truly sick and know that they are, who are most welcome in the presence of such a God. Authority to forgive sins, authority to command repentance and authority to invite all whom he will. Now authority to do what he wishes with the sacred sabbath in a manner which expresses a deeper understanding of the purpose of the giver, than the legalistic Pharisees have ever been able to understand. 'The sabbath was made for man', and even more startling, 'so the Son of man is lord even of the sabbath' (Mark 2:27–28).

The breathless story continues as Jesus meets head-on the combined attacks of religious and political leaders, gathers immense crowds in every part of the nation, sends demonic powers reeling before him and appoints twelve apostles to exercise similar authority themselves. He throws out the challenge to those who meet him that their attitude towards his own claims, and his own work, reveals what their attitude is to the Holy Spirit and God himself (Mark 3:13–35).

Faith and how it works

In the second cycle of stories from chapters 4, 5 and 6 the challenge to faith and the implications of the identity of Jesus are pressed upon us. A clutch of parables present that challenge directly to us; what do we do with the word that is pressed upon us with all its implications for Jesus and the Kingdom of God? Then in another breathless succession of stories, which delight every alliterative preacher, we see Jesus, in turn, expressing his conquest over disaster, demonism, disease and death as he calms the storm that is sinking his boat, casts a legion of demons out of a wretched lunatic, brings to an end years of embarrassment and defilement for a sick woman, and then raises from death a child who has just been snatched from her grieving parents.

Yet in the midst of all of these faith-creating incidents there is a curious reticence, almost an air of secrecy. 'Who then is this?' the disciples cry as they watch the calm fall upon the storm-tossed lake – but they do not provide us with an answer. The once wretched demoniac, now clothed and in his right mind, attempts to follow Jesus but is told to go home. The staggered relatives of the little girl seeing her raised from death naturally wish to tell everyone about it but, 'he strictly charged them that no one should know this' (Mark 5:43). It is a theme of secrecy which will become more evident in the third cycle of stories.

But first Jesus returns to his own town and there is met with incredulity and rejection. Before long the puppet-king of the province has heard of Jesus' fame but draws quite ridiculous conclusions from it (Mark chapter 6).

A question of identity

The third cycle of stories rapidly brings us to the first great climax of Mark's Gospel (the second being of course the crucifixion and resurrection). Jesus takes his disciples outside of the borders of the 'Holy Land' and confronts them with the question 'Who do you say that I am?'. Peter gives the splendidly correct answer, 'You are the Christ', and Jesus forbids his disciples to tell anyone about it (Mark 8:27–30). He is indeed the Christ, but it is not time to say so. Instead, he astounds them with a new teaching about suffering, rejection, death and…resurrection (Mark 8:27–31). A stunningly supernatural event follows, when the Shekinah-glory of God glows from Jesus' being, and a voice from heaven declares his divine Sonship. Again the disciples are told to keep it secret. Not until after the resurrection will any of this make sense! (Mark 9:1–10). Another tremendous scene follows, when the glory of the 'holy mount' is exchanged for the squalor, darkness, demonism and fear of the valley, and the Son of God again displays his authority and compassion.

From now onwards, the miracles almost cease. The great confrontation in Jerusalem will follow, with the climax of cross and empty tomb.

What is Mark saying?
The gospel (good news) is Jesus himself. Mark's very first words tell us so. Having promised to tell us the gospel, he gives us, not a doctrine but a Person. You must decide what to make of this Person, he goes on to say. What Jesus *did,* proclaimed who he *was* – for those with eyes to see and ears to hear. Miracles are what happened when people believed in Jesus. True. But there was always a choice of what to make of the miracles and what to do with Jesus. Nazareth was offended, the Pharisees were unimpressed, Herod could not see it. It is possible to say that miracles happened when people believed in Jesus, but it took faith in Jesus to perceive that miracles were indeed happening. To faith, miracles became signs. They proclaimed the identity and the authority of the Son of God.

What, then, does Mark lead us to? Jesus' final post-resurrection commission to his disciples tells us. They are to go out and announce the forgiveness of sins in his name. Faith receives it. Unbelief shuts the door on it. Nor need there be any confusion about the essential nature of the message. It is not, 'Look at these wonders', but 'Look at Jesus – and believe'. The dramatic promise which follows (omitted from some manuscripts) does not really alter this. The exorcisms, new tongues, safety from serpents and poison, and the healings, are not the essentials of the message but the 'signs' which 'confirmed the message'. Like the earlier signs in Jesus' ministry, they are capable of more than one explanation, and can produce more than one reaction. We shall see later that when Paul cast out a demon, some believed and some thrust him in prison (Acts 16:16–24). When Christians spoke in those tongues, some were impressed and some thought they were drunk (Acts 2:1–13). When Paul shook off a poisonous snake some listened to the gospel but others imprisoned him again (Acts 28:1–6). When missionaries healed a lame man they were mistaken for heathen gods (Acts 14:8–20).

Curiously, this brings us round in full circle to Peter's gospel-proclamation in the Roman military household at Caesarea (Acts 10:34–43). Limited-thinking is entrenched in Peter's mind. He cannot be persuaded to press the offer of salvation on non-Jews. It takes a vision from God (followed by a striking coincidence in the arrival of the Centurion's request) to persuade him that he must not dismiss as 'unclean' those on whom God has set his seeking and saving love. Once he has grasped that 'God shows no partiality', he plunges into an enthusiastic account of Jesus' life, ministry, death and resurrection (one which we have seen closely resembles the outline of Mark's Gospel).

His message draws an immediate and astonishing response, not only from his hearers, but from God. 'The Holy Spirit fell on all who heard the word… they heard them speaking in tongues and extolling God.' Here is one of the 'signs following' promised in Mark's disputed ending. Here, too, is the purpose of the sign. In Mark's words, the gospel is indeed for 'all the world' and addressed to 'the whole creation' (Mark 16:15). In Peter's own words, 'If then God gave the same gift to them as he gave to us when we believed in the Lord Jesus Christ, who was I that I could withstand God?' (Acts 11:17).

We shall return to this scene, for it is full of important principles. Suffice to say that Peter neither expected nor suggested nor offered the supernatural sign. To do so would have destroyed the purpose. It came from God: sovereign, unexpected, totally dependent on divine initiative. That is what made its message irresistible. God was at work where his servants hesitated. To turn the incident into a pattern of normal evangelism (less still of 'second blessing' for Christians) is to miss the whole point of it.

Matthew and Israel's Messiah

If Mark probably wrote for Romans, then Matthew quite certainly wrote for Jews. From the very first verse, (son of David, son of Abraham) and the very first story (wise men journeying to Bethlehem, David's royal city, with the enquiry 'Where is he who has been born King of the Jews?' Matthew 2:2), Matthew is clearly speaking to Israel.

He presents Christ's teaching in five great discourses: Sermon on the Mount (Matthew chapters 5–7); charge to apostles (chapter 10); parables of the Kingdom (chapter 13); humility (chapter 18); the last days (chapters 24–25); each finishing with the same formula. They are clearly meant to remind the reader of the five books of Moses. The Sermon on the Mount, the transfiguration on another mount and the ascension from a third mount, are reminders of Moses who brought God's commands from the holy mountain. The message is obvious. Here is the greater Moses, announcing more spiritual commandments, creating a new Israel. Between these discourses are blocks of writing in which Matthew gathers, in an easily memorized manner, highly effective accounts of the miraculous ministry of Jesus (*e.g.* chapters 8–9). Here, in word and deed, is the Messiah of God.

Another mark of the Jewish appeal is Matthew's constant use of the phrase, 'Then was fulfilled what was spoken by the prophet...', followed by an Old Testament quotation. Some of the references to modern ears sound decidedly odd. For example, Joseph and Mary's return from Egypt with the young child Jesus, is quoted as a 'fulfilment' of Israel's exodus from the same land fourteen hundred years earlier (Matthew 2:13–15). Or, the sorrow in Bethlehem after Herod's massacre of the babies, is offered as a 'fulfilment' of a text from the book of Jeremiah connected with the destruction of Jerusalem by the Babylonians in the sixth century BC (Matthew 2:16–18). It is a typical Jewish thought. Not every reference quoted is regarded as direct forecasting or foretelling (though some are, for example the birth of the Messiah in Bethlehem). More often the writer is simply asserting that the same principles behind one event work their way through and are fulfilled in the second event, because God's purposes are being worked out and God knows all.

So in the Bethlehem example, Matthew sees, in the bitter sorrow of the bereaved mothers over their murdered children, a continuation, and in that sense a fulfilment, of the sorrow of mothers and children dragged into exile and perhaps bereaved of their husbands, under the onslaught of the Babylonian invader in Jeremiah's day. Jeremiah himself in those events had seen an echo of Rachel's lament a thousand years earlier as the great ongoing spiritual conflict, between those who are consciously involved in God's will, and those who are not, found expression. The Hosea and Jeremiah references were not predictions. Rather they were prophetic; they declared a word from God in an ongoing situation. This is important because some of the

103

distinctive contributions Matthew makes to our discussion of the supernatural and the miraculous, revolve round this way of understanding.

The writer, then, is pointing to Jesus, son of Abraham, son of David, Son of God, declared by mighty word and mighty deed. But does he throw light on what it means today to say that he is our Saviour and that he is, 'the same yesterday, today and for ever'?

Jesus – touched by our sorrows

In the first great cycle of incidents (significantly, when Jesus comes down from the mountain; echoes of Moses!) Christ plunges into a number of miraculous healings which are individually recounted and then spends an evening in which, 'they brought to him many who were possessed with demons; and he cast out the spirits with a word, and healed all who were sick.' Then the writer makes the striking comment, 'This was to fulfil what was spoken by the prophet Isaiah, "He took our infirmities and bore our diseases"' (Matthew 8:17). He is referring of course to the classic fifty-third chapter of Isaiah and specifically to verse four. What does he mean?

Some Christians committed to a modern healing ministry have suggested an idea that is summed up in the phrase, 'there is healing in the atonement'. The reasoning goes something like this. In Isaiah's famous chapter, the verse immediately following that quoted by Matthew goes on to say,

> But he was wounded for our transgressions,
>   he was bruised for our iniquities;
> upon him was the chastisement that made us whole,
>   and with his stripes we are healed.

Verse 6 is perhaps even more striking,

All we like sheep have gone astray;
we have turned every one to his own way;
and the Lord has laid on him
the iniquity of us all.

Certainly these two verses present us with a tremendous picture of Calvary. If then verse 4 of the prophecy also refers to Calvary, then, coupling it with Matthew's use of the words, we have the idea that on the cross Christ bore sin *and* sorrow *and* sickness. Then (same reason) since we claim forgiveness by faith, knowing that our sin has been dealt with at the cross, so we can claim healing by faith knowing that our sicknesses have been dealt with at the cross.

Perhaps so. But such an understanding leads to real difficulties of exegesis, of theology, and of practice. What can we *mean* by saying that Jesus, 'carried sickness on the cross'? The New Testament makes abundantly clear what is meant by Jesus carrying our *sin* upon the cross. It involved God: for our sake, 'he made him to be sin who knew no sin' (2 Corinthians 5:20–21). It involved Jesus who had never sinned, having become a curse for us (Galatians 3:10–14). It involved Christ paying the price of our redemption with his own blood (Romans 3:21–25). The New Testament gives no similar statements about the bearing of our sickness on the cross, nor is there any record of such being preached by the apostles. They preached Christ and undoubtedly they performed miracles which had the effect of drawing people's attention to Christ, but nowhere do we find them teaching a theology of Christ bearing our sicknesses.

What then does the quotation mean? Most likely something like this. Jesus, who came in compassion to save us from our sin and from all that springs from it, shared with the most obvious physical consequences of the fall, and in his self-giving, healing ministry was in reality suffering with us. Thus today he is able to 'sympathize with our weaknesses' (Hebrews 4:14–16). Now Isaiah 53 becomes a prophetic description of the whole life of Jesus, not exclusively of his death. So we see his childhood and growth in an unlikely environment ('like a young plant and a root out of dry ground'). We see his rejection by the majority ('he was despised and rejected'). We see his healing ministry, identifying himself with mankind's suffering ('he has borne our griefs and carried our sorrows'). We see his atoning death ('wounded for our transgressions and bruised for our iniquities'). We read of his burial ('his grave with the wicked and with the rich man in his death'). We witness his triumph over death ('he shall see his offspring, he shall prolong his days... I will divide him a portion with the great, and he shall divide the spoil with the strong.')

The sign of Jonah
On two occasions Matthew tells us of enigmatic answers which Jesus gave to religious leaders who demanded a 'sign'. They are chapter 12:38–42, and chapter 16:1–4. In both cases he dismisses the request briskly.

> No sign shall be given...except the sign of the prophet Jonah. For as Jonah was three days and three nights in the belly of the whale, so will the Son of man be three days and three nights in the heart of the earth.

And again,

> An evil and adulterous generation seeks for a sign, but no sign shall be given to it except the sign of Jonah.

Jesus, sadly has been pondering the failure of the cities of Galilee to take his ministry seriously enough to turn in repentance, and prepare themselves for the Kingdom of God. The great privilege that is theirs in hearing him will worsen the judgment that will fall upon them, making it 'more tolerable on the day of judgment for Tyre and Sidon than for you', and 'more tolerable on the day of judgment for the land of Sodom than for you.' They have seen signs enough, they have heard words enough, but because their attitude is wrong then their response to deed and word is bound to be wrong too. So now he turns down this demand for a sign. What kind of sign can possibly convince them, if they are not persuaded by his deeds and his words?

The link with Jonah therefore becomes obvious. The classic story of Jonah is the great Old Testament example of a message of mercy (springing admittedly from a prior message of judgment) being addressed to a pagan nation outside of the covenant and promises of God. Nineveh believed and repented. They did so because of the preaching of Jonah, and because of the remarkable story he had to tell of the determination of God to bring a prophetic warning to the city in time to precipitate their repentance. What greater incentive could Nineveh have, what greater argument urging them to repentance, than the remarkable fact that God had moved heaven and earth (literally!) to ensure that warning and gospel were brought to them? It even involved the disobedient prophet Jonah going through an experience of near death and of apparent resurrection.

The point of the comparison with Jesus now becomes obvious. Already the Son of God is bringing the message in word and deed of the Kingdom of God and the call to repentance. He who brings that message will soon present the further authorization of his deliverance from death and his triumphant emerging from the grave. It is another fascinating example of Matthew's familiar use of the Old Testament. God always works in the same way because eternal principles are always applicable. And by doing so he underlines once again the real purpose and the real crux of the ministry of Jesus whether it be in his preaching or in his deeds of wonder and compassion. The point of it all is to call people to repentance and to bring them back to God.

The promised presence

A very different emphasis is shown in the discourse on humility and forgiveness (chapter 18). It gives us another clue as to what it means today to have the presence of Jesus, the same yesterday, today and for ever. It is one of only two direct references by name to *the church* in the gospel narratives. It is the great promise that makes the Christian church the unique creation that it is. It is no mere club or company or collection of people drawn together by common interests or purposes. It is the people who know among themselves the presence of the living Christ.

> For where two or three are gathered in my name, there am I in the midst of them (verse 20).

Interestingly there is no reference here to the working of miracles. What we see is the outworking of a fellowship of committed people; committed to their Lord and to each other. As such they deal solemnly with persistent and stubborn quarrelling which denies the reality of a forgiven and forgiving company (verses 15–17). They make their decisions of policy with an acute awareness that eternal issues are involved and that there will be consequences in heaven and earth (verse 18). They engage in prayer as a holy exercise that harmonizes their spirits with one another and invokes the help of the living God (verse 19). All this, because Christ is in the midst of those who gather in his name; that is, who act consistently with his character and express his authority.

Of course it cannot possibly be argued that this will *not* involve the miraculous. In a sense it involves the greatest miracle of all. But 'miracle ministry' is not at all the main thrust of the passage. What it means for Christ to be amongst us in living reality today is for the quality of our fellowship to be guarded, the decisions we make to be guided, the prayers we offer to be eagerly energized, and the presence of Jesus to be joyfully welcomed.

The Great Commission

One more example teaches us very much the same thing again. It is what the Duke of Wellington called, 'the marching orders of the Christian church' given by Jesus immediately before his ascension as the disciples gathered around him on, note, 'the mountain to which he had directed them.' The words are famous; the energizing principle behind all evangelistic and missionary endeavour.

> All authority in heaven and on earth has been given to me. Go therefore and make disciples of all nations…and lo, I am with you always, to the close of the age (28:18–20).

The promised presence of Jesus, the same as in Galilee and Jerusalem is to be dependent upon, and expressed within, obedience to the command to take his gospel to all nations. It is the evangelist (surely using that word in the broadest and simplest possible sense) who· can be certain of an experience of the presence of the living Christ. So it proves to be again and again. It is very similar to the ending of Mark's Gospel.

The master who here promises to be with his witnesses, there works with them with signs following. Here the signs are not mentioned. The reason is obvious. The really crucial thing is not the outward sign, the working of wonders, but the message which they illustrate, illuminate and underline. Without doubt as we shall see, the first witnesses did find their proclamation was accompanied by remarkable signs but they were never confused about the purpose of those wonders; it was to declare and confirm the message of salvation through the Lord Jesus Christ and for the confirming and declaring of the gospel which was brought in his name.

John's Gospel – Son of God and source of life

It is obvious to the most casual reader that the Gospel according to John has a very different presentation from Matthew or Mark. It is, in the best sense of that word, the most *artificially* shaped gospel narrative. In his last chapter but one John explains what he has done. Very many things have been done and said by Jesus. John has carefully selected a few with a deliberate purpose in mind. It is to convince people that Jesus Christ is the Son of God so that by faith in his name they might have eternal life (John 20:30-31). He does this by taking a very small number of incidents, carefully recreates their context and circumstances, and then links them with a long discourse from the lips of Jesus in which the deepest meaning of that incident is underlined and applied.

The same pattern constantly repeats itself. It can be summed up alliteratively in the three words, *revelation, rejection,* and *reception*. Again and again Jesus performs a deed which has clear significance, explained and underlined by him in powerful words. That is the *revelation*. Almost invariably he is met by incredulity or doubt or outright opposition on the part of the majority. That is *rejection*. But there are almost always those who respond to the power of the appeal that he is making. That is *reception*. The classic words from the first chapter give the pattern for the whole book.

He came to his own home, (revelation)
and his own people received him not. (rejection)
But to all who received him, who believed in his name,

he gave power to become children of God. (reception) (John 1:11–12)

To produce this pattern John records no more than seven miracles in detail, only two of which overlap with the accounts in Matthew, Mark and Luke. All of them are set in the context of human need, though the need varies enormously from the comparative triviality of a wedding reception running short of wine for the guests, right through to the enormous climax of need for a man who has lain in his tomb for four days.

In almost every case there is a direct and obvious connection between the work of mercy that is brought in power to some needy individual, and a great declaration of an eternal principle that applies to everyone. So, for example, the healing of the paralysed man at the Bethzatha Pool, is made to illustrate the fact that, 'the Son gives life to whom he will' (John 5:1–9, 19–21). The feeding of the five thousand with a few loaves and fish leads to the powerful declaration of Jesus, 'I am the bread of life; he who comes to me shall not hunger, and he who believes in me shall never thirst' (John 6:1–12, 35–36).

With rather more complicated treatment in another three chapters, the claim of Jesus to be the light of the world who brings deliverance from darkness to all who follow him, is *followed* by his healing of a blind man (John 8:12; 9:1–7). The treatment then meted out to this newly enlightened man by the hard and cynical religious authorities, leads Jesus in turn to contrast himself with them as the good shepherd who truly guides and cares for his sheep, as they have so signally failed to do (John 9:24–29; 10:1-6). And in the powerful climax of Christ's ministry, the raising of Lazarus from the dead leads to the great assertion, 'I am the resurrection and the life; he who believes in me, though he die, yet shall he live, and whoever lives and believes in me shall never die' (John 11:1-27).

In contrast to the Synoptic Gospels, in which we see Jesus hesitating or refusing to give 'signs' to those who seek them for quite the wrong reasons and are unimpressed by the greatest sign of all (that is his own life and ministry) this Gospel shows us Jesus deliberately drawing attention to his life and ministry, explaining their significance so that they do indeed become signs. They illustrate and enforce three particular things; his own mission, the salvation that he brings, and his unique relationship with the Father. And they all demand the decision of faith. 'If I am not doing the works of my Father, then do not believe me; but if I do them, even though you do not believe me, believe the works, that you may know and understand that the Father is in me and I am in the Father' (John 10:37–38).

Signs of certainty

In fact the word *signs* so constantly used in this Gospel is the choice of the writer, whereas the favourite on the actual lips of Jesus himself is '*works*'. The word (*ergon*) is used by Jesus no less than seventeen times. These works underline the close association that there is between the Father and the Son, they declare and manifest the character of God, and they bear eloquent testimony to the reality of the words that accompany the works.

The word which John himself prefers to use in describing Christ's miracles is the familiar word '*sign*' but now used much more heavily and much more positively than in the other gospels. So the turning of water into wine is the first sign that Jesus performed, the healing of an official's child at a distance is the second sign and so on. When we come to the final summary of the whole book John makes it quite clear that he has selected only a few out of the many signs which Jesus performed, and that his purpose in so doing is to bring his readers to faith. So faith becomes the central point of the signs. In some cases witnessing a miracle leads to faith and therefore becomes a sign in that sense;

in other cases John is obviously saying that the admiring believer, looking back at these events with the after-thought of faith, can now indeed see them to be signs.

There is a third rather special word which is employed in this Gospel. It is the word *glory* (*doxa*). It is very closely associated with signs, perhaps most strikingly in the words 'This (the turning of water into wine) the first of his signs, Jesus did at Cana in Galilee, and manifested his glory; and his disciples believed in him' (John 2:11). It is the Greek version of the Hebrew word often used in the Old Testament to describe a manifestation of God in some visible form or appearance. John is telling us that the most total and final and complete manifestation of God is in the person of Jesus. 'And the Word became flesh and dwelt among us, full of grace and truth; we have beheld his glory, glory as of the only Son from the Father.' Developing the thought, John goes on to explain, 'No-one has ever seen God: the only Son, who is in the bosom of the Father, he has made him known' (John 1:14, 18).

Glory is what God possesses by the very fact of what and who he is. Or using it in the other sense, we give God glory when we recognize and acknowledge what he is. Since Jesus is the perfect incarnation of God, he embodies within himself the whole of the divine glory. Therefore to honour him is to honour the Father and vice versa.

So the true purpose of 'signs' in John's thinking is clearly seen. Why does Jesus in the Synoptic Gospels seem to discourage or refuse signs whilst John builds up his whole case around them? Because the signs which religious leaders, sensation-seeking crowds and a bored king demanded could prove nothing *per se*. There were always two possible explanations. They did not compel faith in those who had no wish to believe. But John, writing to believers or to those who are willing to find faith, sees signs from another angle. To the eye of dawning faith, Christ's words, deeds and character combine to say, 'This man can give you life.

113

This is the Son of God. He is worthy of your total trust.'

For this reason, too, the spiritual truth behind the signs matter more than the physical fact of the signs. Christ's ability to give new life and hope really *is* a more important and permanent fact than his healing of a lame man at the pool of Bethzatha (John 5:8–9 *cf.* verse 21). Christ's ability to feed the soul with living bread really *does* matter more than his miraculous feeding of a crowd by the Galilee lake (John 6:11, *cf.* verse 51). The glorious words of comfort, certainty and expectation spoken at the grave of every Christian really *do have* more significance than one staggering act of power at a tomb of Bethany (John 11:43, *cf.* verse 25). I have taken parties of wondering and worshipping Christians to what are almost certainly the authentic sites of these miracles. But the greater wonder was their own worship. Here were people of widely differing temperaments, backgrounds and experiences. I had already seen them turn from unbelief, bereavement, despair, to embrace by faith a living Christ and to find life in him. That is what the 'signs' are for, and that is what they signify.

> Jesus did many other signs …these are written that you may believe that Jesus is the Christ, the Son of God, and that believing you may have life in his name (John 20:30–31).

Greater works than these

We come now to possibly the most remarkable words of Jesus recorded by John. He was nearing his moment of supreme suffering and sacrifice. He was appealing once more to his words, his works and his authority. Then came the startling promise.

> Truly, truly, I say to you, he who believes in me will also do the works that I do; and greater works than

these will he do, because I go to the Father (John 14:12).

The works that he does? *Greater* works than he does? What can this possibly mean? What can today's church look for and expect that can remotely be regarded as equal to and exceeding his own deeds of power? How is such a promise matched in the placid worship of the Parish Church at evensong, or the tea-and-buns of the Free Church women's fellowship?

There are several possible meanings:

Geographically wider works. Jesus never travelled more than fifty miles outside the provinces of Galilee and Judea, obscure and tiny outposts of the Roman Empire. Today, his name is revered and acts of compassion performed in continents undreamt of in the first century. Is this the 'greater' work?

More numerous works. Jesus left perhaps a thousand 'converts'. (There were certainly five hundred witnesses to his resurrection, 1 Corinthians 15:3–7). Yet three thousand were swept into the church by Peter's anointed preaching on the Day of Pentecost. A modern mass evangelist may see that many 'decisions' at one gospel rally. A missionary society in West Africa or an independent church in Asia will report more conversions in a year. Billy Graham has preached the gospel to more people face-to-face than populated the whole known world of the gospel narratives. Jesus healed several lepers; we might guess at perhaps fifty. Who can count how many have been healed by the ministry of the Leprosy Mission? Who can measure the pioneer work of Christian hospitals in lands where medical care scarcely existed until the Christians came?

More universal works. Although Christ's heart was open to all, with scarcely an exception, his ministry took him only

115

to Jews. The breaking of all barriers of race and culture came in the subsequent ministry of the apostles. The same gospel was preached and the same miracles performed on a universal scale which was seen to be the most glorious confirmation of Christ's message (Acts 15:12; Ephesians 2:11–13).

More wonderful works. The words, if they stood alone, could be understood as implying more astonishing miracles, and more marvellous experiences of the intervention of God. This would imply that they were *qualitatively* greater. Some enthusiastic Christians have not hesitated to say so. The Church, they claim, should live in the constant expectation and experience of miracles as astonishing as (and more astonishing than) the miracles of Jesus. In actual fact it is difficult to see how this can be. 'The works that I do' – yes, perhaps. But how can there be 'greater works'? What can be more for a lame man than to walk? What miracle performed on a blind man can exceed the wonder of receiving sight? Above all, what greater thing can you do to a dead man than to bring him to life? All of these miracles have perhaps been *repeated* from time to time in the experience of the Church, but how can they be *exceeded*?

Different works which by their nature are even more wonderful. This is how the promise has normally been understood in the 'main line' of Christian thinking. Origen (185-254) wrote in his usual vivid and allegorical manner,

> According to the promise of Jesus the disciples have done greater works than the physical miracles which Jesus did. For the eyes of people blind in soul are always being opened, and the ears of those who were deaf to any talk of virtue eagerly hear about God and the blessed life with him. Many too who were lame in the feet of

116

their inner man...receive from Jesus power to walk on their feet...over all the power of the enemy.[2]

Athanasius (296–373) asserted that the 'greatest sign' is the moral change that causes a girl to preserve her purity, a youth to live in continence, an idolator to turn to Christ.[3]

In a splendid passage, John Chrysostom (344–407) argued that spiritual sight is a 'better sign' than physical healing of the blind. It is a 'greater work' to be ready to die for your faith than to raise the dead, and to despise money as grass rather than to turn grass into money.[4]

This final remark recalls to my mind a breezy character from London dockland who was converted to Christ on a race-course. The change erased from his life the habit of drunkenness which had impoverished his family and denuded his house. Now it was so different; a happy family and a decently furnished home. He used to claim in open-air meetings, 'Once Christ turned water into wine; now he turns beer into furniture.'

Protestant thinking has continued this interpretation. The 'greater work' is not merely more widespread; it is greater in kind. *The new birth* is the most radical, fundamental and supernatural evidence of Christ's power, to which the physical miracles of his earthly ministry are but pointers and parables. Bishop J.C. Ryle, the first Bishop of Liverpool, wrote,

> The meaning of these words must be sought in the moral and spiritual miracles which followed the preaching of the apostles...We read of no apostle walking on water, or raising a person four days dead. What our Lord has in view seems to be the far greater number of *conversions*, the far wider spread of the Gospel. In short, 'greater works' means more conversions. There is no greater work possible than the conversion of a soul.[5]

Charles Spurgeon, the great Victorian Baptist preacher said,

> Those works of the Holy Spirit which are at this time vouchsafed to the Church of God are every way as valuable as those earlier miraculous gifts...the work by which men are quickened from their death in sin, is not inferior to the power which made men speak with tongues.[6]

William Hendriksen, the modern Reformed commentator says the same.

> Christ's works had consisted to a considerable extent of miracles in the physical realm, performed largely among the Jews. When he now speaks about *the greater works*, he is in all probability thinking of those in connection with *the conversion of the Gentiles*....the greater works are the *spiritual* works.[7]

The cross and the empty tomb
Of course Jesus did not make this much-quoted promise in a vacuum. It comes as the climax of a sustained argument. The subject at the beginning of John chapter 14 is his imminent departure from the disciples, by way of the cross. They are not to be grieved and distressed; his going will 'prepare a place' for them, where he and they shall be forever with the Father (verses 1–7).

Philip naively asks to see the Father. 'Then we shall be satisfied'. Modest request! Jesus is disappointed. 'Have I been with you so long, and yet you do not know me, Philip? He who has seen me has seen the Father' (verses 8–10). Whatever Philip dimly imagined he needed to see (even more power displayed? Even more spectacular signs?) he was looking in the wrong direction. God's *character* is his supreme glory (not his power). All of God's character that can be compressed into a human life was seen in Jesus; to see him was to see God in the only way that God can be seen by human eyes.

The works and words of Christ combine to 'show us the Father'. The perfect accord between Father and Son guarantees that this is so (verse 11). So the Master has come to the subject of his 'works' and those which will be done by those who believe in him. 'The works that I do, and greater works than these'; that is the marvellous prospect (verse 12). What is the basis for such a promise? The very subject which began the discussion.

... because I go to the Father (John 14:12)

Their loss of Jesus will be the gain of the disciples! For that 'loss', that 'going to the Father', is the glory beyond the suffering of the cross and the wonders of the empty tomb. At the right hand of God, in the fullness of his power, the enthroned Saviour answers the prayers of his people.

Whatever you ask in my name, I will do it (verse 13)

Not only so. Another consequence of the ascension will be *the coming of the Holy Spirit*.

I will pray the Father, and he will give you another Counselor, to be with you for ever, even the Spirit of truth, whom the world cannot receive (verses 16–17).

Now it is clear. The 'greater works' are the consequences of a gospel made possible by the cross, confirmed by the resurrection, preached universally in the power of the Holy Spirit. Those three events, crucifixion, rising and outpoured Spirit, were necessary before the 'greater works' could be performed. Anything following naturally from these greatest acts in God's plan of salvation must of necessity be 'greater' than anything that preceded them. What followed in fact was the transformation of lives produced by a Spirit-empowered proclamation of the gospel which led to the building and expansion of the church.

The outpoured Spirit

And all hinged on that 'going away' without which there could be no outpoured Spirit. Jesus would say it again that same evening,

> …it is to your advantage that I go away (16:7).

Their *advantage*? How could anything be better, more advantageous, more in their interest, than to have the physical presence of their Master, to hear his words, to see his face, to witness his mighty works? This is how.

> …if I do not go away, the Counselor will not come to you; but if I go I will send him to you. And when he comes, he will convince the world… (verses 7–8).

Absent Christ (physically) means present Spirit. Through his crucifixion, resurrection and bodily return to heaven, Christ is released spiritually, so to speak, so that his presence may be known everywhere to all. Until then, if he was in Capernaum he could not be in Jerusalem; if in Jerusalem then absent from Caesarea. After Pentecost, he was everywhere at once; wherever his disciples went; wherever his gospel was proclaimed. He revealed himself to Jews in Jerusalem, to despised outcasts in Samaria and to Romans in Caesarea by outpoured Spirit, 'as on us at the beginning' as the delighted Peter exclaims.

Ever since, it has gone on 'as at the beginning'. The spreading presence of Christ by his Spirit which within a generation had reached the cities and towns of the Roman

Mediterranean world, is today realized in Tokyo and Peking, in Zimbabwe and Zaire, in Moscow and Murmansk, in London and New York. Matthew's 'Lo I am with you always', and Mark's 'Everywhere the Lord worked with them' is realized and explained by John's 'If I go I will send him to you'.

This is, of course, precisely the order of events in our alone divinely-inspired church history, *the Acts of the Apostles*. Acts 1 and 2 describe the existential reality of John 14 theology-and-promise.

Here is the reiterated call to world-wide mission

...you shall be my witnesses in Jerusalem... and to the end of the earth (1:8).

Here is the repeated promise of the spiritual presence

...you shall receive power when the Holy Spirit has come upon you (1:8).

Here is the departure of Jesus

...when he had said this, as they were looking on, he was lifted up, and a cloud took him out of their sight (1:9).

Here is the 'better thing', greatly to their advantage, in the going away of Jesus

...they were all filled with the Holy Spirit (2:4).

Here is the first announcement of a gospel greater in scope than ever before imagined

...the promise is to you and to your children and to all that are far off, every one whom the Lord our God calls to him (2:39).

121

Here is the first foretaste of those 'greater works' which now begin

…there were added that day about three thousand souls (2:41).

This survey has brought us out of the gospel records and into the story of the Early Church. But there is another Gospel still to examine. Properly, however, it belongs to *The Acts of the Apostles* in a special way. For Luke's two-volume work, Gospel and Acts, takes us right to the heart of the matter. It is, uniquely, the story of the work of the Holy Spirit before and after the ministry of Jesus. It answers, more clearly than any other part of the Bible, the question, *'What does it mean today that Jesus is always the same?'*

To that we now turn.

Notes for chapter six

[1] Papias, a disciple of John, first referred to this tradition, calling Mark 'Peter's secretary' and the Gospel 'Peter's memoirs'.

[2] Origen – *Contra Celsum* 2:48

[3] Athanasius *Ephesians* 49:7

[4] Chrysostom, *Hom, in Matthew* 32:11

[5] J.C. Ryle, *Expository Thoughts on St. John* (J. Clarke, 1954).

[6] C.H. Spurgeon, *Metropolitan Tabernacle Pulpits 1884,* Vol. 30, (Banner of Truth, 1971), p.386.

[7] William Hendriksen, *The Gospel of John* (Banner of Truth, 1959).

7

Church triumphant

I recall an amusing and powerful sketch presented by a group of my church's young people. They pictured a teenager showing his friend the interior of the church where he had become a Christian. How such a conversion had come about was something of a mystery. For the church was sadly lacking in any certainty about the authority of the Bible and the reality of the supernatural. The Christian's friend plied him with dismissive objections and questions as they sat together on the chancel steps. And to each one the Christian surrendered without firing a shot.

'Genesis? Oh well, of *course* I'm not expected to believe that. No, I don't give up my scientific training. Genesis is a book of myths... Noah's flood? Well of *course* they couldn't have rounded up giraffes and rhinoceri. No, it is a pious fable with a moral to it... Elisha's miracles? Well, it was a simple age, and he probably combined a bit of folk medicine with some happy coincidences to point out spiritual truths. It's the *truth* that matters, you see, not the *story*... Jesus feeding five thousand people with a boy's picnic? Well this writer I've come across suggests that many of the people had *their* picnics with them too, but didn't like to share them. Then when the boy gave his bread and fish to Jesus they all felt ashamed, so they shared theirs as well. The *moral* you see, that's what matters.... Peter escaping from prison with the help of an angel? Well, it's literary hyperbole. What it means is that Peter's release was so unexpected that it was *as if* the guards had gone to sleep and an angel had broken the chains.'

Meanwhile (in the sketch) a suitably-robed figure stood unnoticed in the pulpit behind them, holding a large black 'Bible'. And every time another miracle or incident was dismissed, the figure tore out another page from his 'Bible' and dropped it into a waste-paper tin (the tearing noise and the plop in the bin was splendidly amplified through a microphone). At the end of the conversation the 'minister' shrugged and dropped a now-empty black Bible-cover with a final clang into the bin. Meanwhile the Christian concluded... 'So you see it's all very reasonable. I'd love *you* to become a Christian too. How about it?' To which his friend replied witheringly – 'Why on earth *should* I? You haven't got any more than I have! No thanks'... and walked off.

The warning is a necessary one. The 'supernatural' and the 'natural' are so completely intermingled in the Bible that any effort to disentangle the one from the other and accept only the second is doomed to failure. We have seen that it cannot be done with the Old Testament drama and we have seen why. Nor can it be done with the figure of Jesus as drawn by the gospel writers. Words, works and character make one consistent picture. But what of the church as we see it depicted in *the Acts of the Apostles*? The same warning applies. Cut out the special and miraculous, and the remainder will be tattered indeed.

This raises a new question, and it is one constantly and unavoidably raised whenever Christians meet together and act together. Jesus Christ is unique. His 'mighty works' declare that uniqueness. But is the first-generation church unique? Is *Acts* the description of a once-only situation, or a picture of the 'normal Christian church'? Should we expect to see the kind of thing happening *now* that happens on almost every page of that book?

If we *should*, then it would seem that we are looking for a fairly eventful life, to put it mildly. A lame man is healed. Prisoners are released by angels. Miracles persuade a Samaritan community to believe. An opponent of the gospel is struck blind. Evangelists make such an impact that they are mistaken for pagan deities. A vision leads missionaries to enter Europe. The capital of Roman Asia is almost emptied of idol-worshippers as miracles are performed. Is this what we are to expect every day? It makes the average activity of the Parochial Church Council, the Deacons' Meeting, the College C.U. Committee look disconcertingly tame!

Have we gone terribly astray somewhere? Do we stand guilty of respectability, over-organization and lack of faith? Should we be casting out spirits instead of getting out agendas? Have we replaced crusades with committees? Have we settled for bishops and superintendents who keep the religious bureaucracy going, when what we need is apostles and prophets who shake communities and turn the world upside down? Have we entangled our college witness in apologetics when what we need is an earthquake?

Lessons from history

Every so often a movement of protest and renewal bubbles up within the organized church and poses these questions. Montanism was perhaps the first to do so after the apostolic age. From about AD170 and for two hundred years, it registered a protest against worldliness, over-intellectualism and religious respectability. The movement won to its ranks one of the second century's most brilliant churchmen; Tertullian who had coined the famous phrase, 'The blood of the martyrs is the seed of the church'. Montanists gloried in martyrdom, asceticism and vows of chastity. They reinstated prophecy and tongues as regular church activities. They looked for miracles. 'As at the beginning' could well be taken as their motto. They ran into excesses of credulity, rash foretelling and unrestrained emotion. With some hesitations the main-line church rejected them and thereby lost a vigour which it needed and withdrew a calming influence which it could have provided. Most readers will recognize in this story a pattern which has repeated itself throughout Christian history and is not hard to find in today's situation.

Very soon indeed the successors to the apostles seem to have found the subject perplexing. At this remove of time it is not easy to be sure what their own experience was. Some of them talk and act as if *Acts* is being repeated all the time. Others find it necessary to explain why it is no longer happening. Some speak of it happening, but rather less often. This should not surprise us. Let a modern visitor to Britain try to find out what is really happening on the church scene here, and depending on whom he speaks to and where he looks, he will get surprisingly varied answers. Let someone in this country try to get an accurate picture of Christianity in Indonesia without actually going there, and he will find it even more confusing.

Eusebius, the church's first systematic historian, wrote at the end of the third century that 'some small measure' of Christ's power was still being seen in contemporary miracles.[1] Much earlier than that, Justin Martyr in the mid-second century speaks of miraculous gifts 'among us now', and specifically mentions prophecy, healing and exorcism.[2] About the same time Irenaeus describes exorcism ('a standing Christian miracle'), prediction, healing, raising the dead, speaking in tongues, insight into secrets and (curiously) expounding the Scriptures, all as examples of the activities of 'all who were truly disciples of Jesus'. There is an odd switch of tenses when mentioning the raising of the dead, which casts some doubt on whether he meant 'now' (to him) or 'previously' (in apostolic times).[3]

Healing and exorcism seem to have been so regular

phenomena that they can be regarded as normal tools in the evangelism of the early centuries. 'You may learn this from what goes on under your own eyes', argued Justin. 'Many of our Christian men have exorcised in the name of Jesus Christ, numberless demoniacs throughout the whole world, and in your city. When all other exorcists and specialists in incantations and drugs have failed, they have healed…. Others still heal the sick by laying their hands upon them, and they are made whole.'[4]

Augustine

The great Augustine (354–430) lived in the heyday of a church at peace with the empire; powerful, respectable, established, and with the complete Bible in its hand. He seems to have had a certain amount of trouble with the supernatural, sometimes speaking of it as a phenomenon of the past, sometimes claiming it as contemporary. He was confronted by heretics whose claims of the miraculous he could scornfully dismiss as spurious or third-rate in comparison to genuine Christian miracles. At the same time, he was troubled by more orthodox extremists to whom he wished to present the authority of Scripture and the advantages of an ordered church as preferable to constantly living in the world of the wonderful. Does that sound very modern? This (I suggest) accounts for the fact that competing theorists today can quote him with equal effectiveness to support opposing ideas.

In his classic *The City of God* he related, with circumstantial detail, more than twenty miracles he had witnessed, and hinted at ten times as many. He listed a presbyter healed of 'the stone', a boy raised when dying at a road-accident, a blind man given sight. More astonishingly he confidently claimed several examples of the dead restored to life. What is most uncomfortable to a modern Protestant reader is the context. Many of the miracles were connected with the display of the martyr Stephen's bones, discovered (so we learn) in Jerusalem in 415 and some of them sent to North Africa in 424. This was no problem for Augustine. 'Think, beloved, what the Lord must have in store for us in the land of the living, when he bestows so much in the ashes of the dead', he reasoned cheerfully.[5]

After that it is more than a little puzzling to read in his earlier work a defence of the position that only the apostles performed miracles, '–and through them it has been brought about that these should no longer be necessary for their descendants... lest the mind should always seek visible things'. In a splendid piece of logical argument he asks rhetorically, 'Why do not these things take place now?' and replies, 'Because they would not impress unless they were wonderful, and if they were customary they would not be wonderful.'[6]

In later life he found these statements embarrassing. 'What I said is not to be interpreted that no miracles are believed to be performed in the present time. For when I wrote that book, I myself had recently learned that a blind man had been restored to sight.'[7]

What *had* he meant, then? 'Only that none were wrought which were as great as those our Lord wrought, and that not all the kinds our Lord wrought continued to be wrought'.

It is all very puzzling. Protestant thinking has tended to quote the confusion as evidence of two important facts. Genuinely apostolic miracles have disappeared, as they were meant to do. Superstitious Roman Catholic practices are beginning to arrive as they should not have done. Certainly both tendencies are seen in many records from that time onwards. The presence of a host of marvels and superstitious wonders in the medieval church caused the Protestant reformers to react almost against the possibility of real miracles.

The Acts of the Apostles

What does this book give us; a blue-print for church life and growth in every age, or a record of a special and unique beginning? To answer that, we have to lay down a few principles which must be applied in getting to grips with this remarkable writing.

We must not rob it of its supernatural content. Acts is a sober account by a cultured man who could be described as a reliable amateur historian. Many of Luke's circumstantial details and casual references have been confirmed by history, geography and archaeology. He carefully sets his story in a recognizable framework which can be cross-checked from non-biblical documents. Local colour and culture, major and minor political characters, little touches that reflect varied customs and traditions, correct titles given to officials in the maze of Roman colonial life; all of these features earn him the title given him by Sir William Ramsay, 'a historian of the first rank'.

Yet totally intermingled with this history is the constant reference to the supernatural. He gives the name of a Roman proconsul – and tells how the man witnessed judgment falling on an opponent of the gospel (13:6-12). He describes the struggle of the town-clerk of Ephesus to keep order in a tense political situation, which contemporary history records, and tells us that this particular riot arose from the threat posed to pagan relic-makers by the preaching and 'extraordinary miracles' of Paul (19:8-10 and 23-41). He details the stoning of Stephen the first martyr, with a wealth of accurate Jewish detail, but climaxes it with a vision of heaven (6:8-15 and 7:47-60). For the Christian it is sufficient, in any case, to remind himself that Luke's writing is part of the Bible. The record stands as one piece. No amount of verbal legerdemain can remove the miraculous. We should not wish to.

We must not exaggerate its supernatural content, either. Acts is *not* in fact a miracle-a-day story. It covers a period of about thirty years. The marvellous events are seen to be spread quite thinly if the whole story is read with historical sensitivity and imagination. These remarkable events are often highlighted precisely because they are remarkable. Interspersed between them are general phrases which suggest quite long periods of 'normal' life and activity.

And the Lord added to their number day by day (2:47).
Every day in the temple and at home they did not cease teaching and preaching (5:42).
So the church throughout all Judea and Galilee and Samaria had peace and was built up (9:31).

Moreover, the 'wonder-stories' are often balanced by perfectly normal incidents. Philip was dramatically guided to bear witness to a foreign politician in an unlikely place (8:26) but Paul began his missionary journeys by following obvious trade-routes and working his way systematically through Cyprus (13:4–6). Peter was marvellously rescued from prison, but James was beheaded in the same jail; no angelic intervention (12:1–11). Far from expecting wonders every day, the Christians at prayer refused to believe that Peter had really been rescued (12:12–17). Faced with a social problem with rather nasty racial overtones, the apostles did not give the laying-on of hands for racial healing, but organized a sensible sub-committee to look after the soup-kitchen (6:1–6). Warned by prophecy of a coming famine, the church leaders did not pray for a miracle, but simply took prudent steps to lay in supplies (11:27–30). The apostles sometimes performed miracles and saw a crowd gather as a result. But their normal method of *looking* for a crowd was to visit the obvious places like synagogue, market-place and debating-hall.

A vision and a startling coincidence resolves Peter's

doubts about sharing the gospel with non-Jews (10:1–23). But similar doubts in Jerusalem were settled rather by prolonged debate, the sifting of evidence and the study of Scripture (15:1–21). The eventual decision at that 'council', so splendidly described as, 'It seemed good to the Holy Spirit and to us' (verse 28) was reached without any apparent intervention of the supernatural.

This point may seem laboured, but it is important. We all love dramatic stories, and easily credit them with disproportionate importance. I recall worshipping in a Baptist Church in Jerusalem and listening to greetings and reports from Christian leaders of various denominations. An Asian Presbyterian leader with dead-pan face and voice reported a year of progress in his area which included (I quote) 'twelve lepers healed, five barren women with child, and two people raised from the dead.' I shall probably never forget it. I have already forgotten a mass of 'normal' facts which were far more numerous and arguably more important; new churches established, pastors appointed, presbyteries organized, teachers trained, nurses qualified, clinics opened, church members welcomed. Of course Luke writing Acts does not do this, but we easily do it when we read Acts – and when we hear about current events.

We must not put it in solitary confinement. Faced by the indisputable marvel of early church life, and embarrassed by the contrast today, we can too easily shut *Acts* away in a special compartment. The most extreme method among some evangelical Christians is to give it a 'dispensation' of its own. Dispensationalism, popularized by J.N.Darby, the originator of one of the branches of Brethrenism, is the attempt to interpret individual Scriptures in the light of their particular era. It recognizes that we must ask of a biblical event or teaching, 'What was God saying and doing *then*?' In itself, that is a healthy exercise. Quite obviously, God's commands to Israel emerging from Egyptian slavery had a particular 'there-and-then' about them. We neither gather manna nor sacrifice a red heifer nowadays. A more fundamental example would be the period of Jesus Christ's earthly ministry. The church was not yet established, the victory of the cross had not yet been achieved, the Holy Spirit had not yet come. The Bible goes out of its way to say so (Matthew 16:18; 17:9; John 7:39).

What one extreme form of dispensationalism does is to imagine *Acts* to be such a temporary and non-recurring period. It is claimed to be an interim period when Christ, having been rejected by his own people, gives them a second chance. His kingdom is, in a sense, set up in Jerusalem after all, in acts of power. Again it is rejected, and the apostles turn their attention to the Gentiles. Some suggest that Acts 13:46 marks the point. 'Since you … judge yourselves unworthy of eternal life, behold, we turn to the Gentiles.' Now (it is reasoned) since 'Jews demand signs', outstanding miracles were vouchsafed to them during this period. Once the Gentile mission was well under way and the Jews increasingly rejected the gospel, miracles and wonders faded from the scene. Since the church's mission today is to Gentiles, we would not expect the miracles to be repeated.

It is a complex and clever argument, but it will not do. To impose two different 'dispensations' on the book of Acts is to tear it apart without justification. It leads to some odd results, which at least some supporters of the theory are quite happy to embrace. For example, baptism and communion are relegated to the early period, along with miracles. As for the 'Jews-demand-a-sign' argument, it curiously misinterprets the reference quoted in 1 Corinthians 1:23. In fact Paul is there characterizing the factors which most impress Jews and Greeks respectively, and emphasizing that *the gospel panders to neither desire*.

Jews demand signs and Greeks seek wisdom, but we preach Christ crucified, a stumbling block to Jews and folly to Gentiles, *but* to those who are called, both Jews and Greeks, Christ the power of God and the wisdom of God. (My italics)

I have heard it argued that 'speaking in tongues' was very prevalent in the church at Corinth (as witness 1 Corinthians 12 and 14) because the Christians met next door to the synagogue (yes, they did – see Acts 18:5–7!) so the Jews who 'demand signs' would hear the sign of tongues and be impressed. I was delighted at the ingenuity, but totally unconvinced by the reasoning! No, the implications of *Acts* cannot be locked away in solitary confinement.

We must not treat it as a temporary situation. Extreme dispensationalism does this, but there are other approaches which have the same effect, and avowedly do so with the same motive (that is, to put the embarrassing supernatural element at one remove from us).

It is sometimes argued that the whole apostolic period was special and temporary *because the Bible was not yet complete*. The Gospels were not written. The first epistles were just being circulated. The truth about the life, death and resurrection of Jesus was passed and preserved by word of mouth, conversation, public worship and evangelistic preaching. The teaching of the apostles, similarly, was given verbally as they travelled from place to place. Thus, it is argued, there was a special need for divine authentication of *the apostles*, who were avowedly and by definition eye-witnesses (Acts 1:21–22 '...who have accompanied us during all the time that the Lord Jesus went in and out among us, beginning from the baptism of John until the day when he was taken up from us... a witness to his resurrection'). So, also, *prophets* were necessary to give by direct revelation the truths not yet formalized and recorded in the

New Testament. Once the 'canon' of Scripture was complete, neither miracle nor prophet was necessary. And how significant indeed that as the second and third century passed, miracle and prophecy declined until by the time the New Testament was gathered and in circulation in the fourth century, they disappeared altogether. So the argument goes.

Again, it is a clever argument, and it raises an important point to which we must return. But can it hold water? Hardly; its lack of clear scriptural statement puts a question mark over it. Some exponents have pointed to Paul's words to the Corinthian converts –

> as for prophecies, they will pass away; as for tongues, they will cease...
> For ... our prophecy is imperfect; but when the perfect comes, the imperfect will pass away (1 Corinthians 13:8-10).

There you are, they argue. Prophecy and tongues, two of the most striking miraculous elements in the early church, will cease. When? Verse 10 tells us – when the complete and perfect arrives and makes the incomplete and imperfect unnecessary. In other words, *when the New Testament is complete*. Henceforth, with a visible objective revelation in black-and-white in our hands, we have no need of the special emergency provision for our faith.

But can the passage really bear that meaning? It must be consistent throughout the argument. We must maintain that the mighty works of the Holy Spirit in the apostolic age were 'childish ways' now left behind (verse 11). We must maintain that Peter's and Paul's listeners saw and heard a poor reflection, as seen in a cheap and inefficient metal mirror of ancient times, whereas the modern reader of the Bible sees perfectly and 'understands fully'. We must maintain that the preaching and exhortations of the apostles and prophets (accompanied by works of power) gave only partial knowledge, but now the reader of the Bible knows everything as fully as he is known to God.

> When I became a man, I gave up childish ways. For now we see in a mirror dimly, but then face to face. Now I know in part; then I shall understand fully, even as I have been fully understood (verses 11-12).

Can Paul really speak unfavourably of the apostolic experience and faith as a poor reflection, compared to the 'real thing' of a future Bible in black and white? His further use of the same mirror-illustration with the same readers surely sets the record straight.

> We all, with unveiled face, beholding the glory of the Lord, are being changed into his likeness from one degree of glory to another (2 Corinthians 3:18).

In other words, our experience and faith is at best a poor reflection, for we are human, limited, frail, and prone to stumble. But the likeness of Christ increases within us as our Christian life goes on. How will it end?

> It does not yet appear what we shall be, but we know that when he appears we shall be like him, *for we shall see him as he is* (1 John 3:2). (My italics)

That surely, is the '*then*' of Paul's expectation, when 'I shall understand fully, even as I have been fully understood' (1 Corinthians 13:12). Not a Bible in the hand but a glorified spirit in heaven is what Paul looks forward to; not a visible New Testament (however vital that indeed is) but a visible Saviour. This is totally consistent with the context of Paul's 'ode to love' in the Corinthian letter. It is *the superiority of love* that he is arguing, not the superiority of a written

135

Bible. That love is the most distinctive mark of the developing Christ-character within the believer. The time when it is complete is the future state of glory, not the future possession of a New Testament (however vital that is).

In fact the canon-of-Scripture argument as an end to the miraculous is a *non-sequitur*. It brings the facts around in an absurd circle. For if the divinely-authenticated ministry of power and truth exercised by apostles and prophets is replaced by the completed Scriptures, what do those Scriptures bring us? Precisely *the teaching of the apostles and prophets*, the details of their divine authentication, and careful instruction in *how to regulate* the miraculous gifts.

This is never more clear than in the whole passage (1 Corinthians chapters 12–14) from which the 'childish ways' argument is lifted. The section of Paul's letter pleads for a right understanding of 'spiritual gifts' (12:1). It lists some of them (12:7–10). It lays down the vital principle behind their distribution.

> To each is given the [different] manifestation of the Spirit for the common good (12:7).

It is a principle which zealous advocates and critics of the charismatic movement could alike give more attention. The Holy Spirit 'apportions to each one individually as he wills' (12:11).

The same passage teaches the best safeguard against the misuse of spectacular gifts. It is an understanding of the church as the body of Christ (12:14–26). It puts jealousy, mock- modesty, self-display and mutual criticism out of court. It makes odious comparisons of different people's gifts a nonsense.

'You are the body of Christ and individually members of it' (12:27). For that reason, gifts are as numerous and as varied as limbs in a body, and there is not one gift of which it can be said, all should teach, all should work miracles, all should speak in tongues or whatever (12:28–30).

In the even more detailed and specific instructions of chapter 14, the image is still the same. The only way to measure the relative importance of one gift over another is to measure its tendency to build up the body and its members rather than to give selfish individual expression, enjoyment and kudos.

Now it is this truth of *the church as the body of Christ* that forms the foundation and framework of the whole discussion. This is clearly a truth for the whole age of the church. This is the area of the working of the supernatural in the church. The permanent truth of the living limbs in the body of Christ, not the temporary fact that something special was needed until the New Testament was complete – *this* is the foundation for understanding the subject. And it is the now-completed canon of Scripture which tells us so.

We must not turn anecdotes into rules. This is the equal and opposite error to some of those already mentioned. If we cannot dismiss the *Acts* stories as *'not for today'*, does this mean that they should be repeated in our lives and in our churches *every day*? Many people would say so. But, pressed to extremes, the expectation either creates havoc and division, plunges the church into experience-based subjectivism, or leads its holders into self-deception and rather pathetic pretence. We can all think of examples.

Division and disorder is bound to come if we turn a few *Acts* stories into rules for today. Here is one familiar argument. 'Whenever the Holy Spirit fell upon people in *Acts*, they spoke in tongues. Here is the infallible sign then, the initial evidence.' This, of course, lifts 'tongues' to an importance which it simply cannot carry, either in modern experience or in Bible teaching.

As a matter of fact the outpoured Spirit did *not* always give tongues as the sign. He did on the Day of Pentecost

(Acts 2:1–4). He did again when Peter first took the gospel to a Roman household (Acts 10:44–46). He worked similarly again when Paul instructed some disciples of a baptizing sect in Ephesus (Acts 19:1–7). It is assumed (without any clear statement) that the same happened to the first Samaritan Christians after Philip's evangelistic visit, since something audible or visible impressed Simon the Sorcerer (Acts 8:14–19). There is not the slightest evidence that the same happened when in Jerusalem 'more than ever believers were added to the Lord' (Acts 5:14) when in Joppa 'many believed in the Lord', (Acts 9:42) or when in Philippi the Roman jailor's whole family and household were converted (Acts 16:29–34).

Good Christian men whom we respect for their love and zeal really should avoid the special pleading and dubious use of Bible texts which argue – (a) in three cases it happened, (b) in one case we assume something rather like it happened, (c) in the other cases we are convinced it happened but was not mentioned, because it always happens, (d) therefore it can be boldly asserted and insisted that it always happened in the Bible and must always happen today.

Interestingly, even the three cases when it undoubtedly 'happened' are not really similar. At Pentecost the gift of tongues came long after conversion, and conceivably could be described as a further step in commitment (though only, I suggest, at the cost of misunderstanding the significance of Pentecost). At Roman Caesarea it happened whilst people not yet Christians were listening to the gospel for the first time (therefore concurrently with conversion and before baptism). In Ephesus it is very difficult to be sure that the 'disciples' were truly Christian until then (knowing nothing of the Holy Spirit's coming, needing to have the gospel explained, and not yet baptized into Christ). In Samaria (if we concede this as a possible example) the recipients were already converted and baptized but something was missing until the apostles visited them.

Where is the pattern here? Certainly there is not a pattern that says: (1) People are converted and baptized; (2) They still lack power until they are filled or baptized with the Spirit; (3) When *that* happens, they speak in tongues as the evidence. The most that can be drawn from these incidents is a principle, not a pattern. The wind of the Spirit blows where it wishes, as Jesus said (John 3:8). The sovereign Spirit bestows gifts upon people as and when and how he chooses, just as he determines, as Paul said (1Corinthians 12:11). Not *unfailing regularity*, but *unrestricted variety* is the picture given.

So much for the biblical confusion which such an argument can cause. The practical consequences will follow. Once impose a rule from anecdotes (in this case, fullness of the Spirit proved by tongues) and division will follow as night follows day. That may very well not be the intention and often it is not. But those who do not speak in tongues will feel (or fear, or even be told) that they are second-class citizens. Some will be discouraged and stumble. Some will redouble desperate efforts to 'get it'. And if we want a thing badly enough we are likely to get it, or get something like it but different, or manufacture something vaguely resembling it. Others will feel impelled to oppose the whole thing, and may well throw out the genuine with the spurious.

All this happens when anecdotes are turned into rules. It is a formula for division, depression, disorder, discouragement and disaster.

We have perhaps laboured this particular example, but everyone knows how important and topical it is. I recently gave Bible studies for teams of German, French and Dutch young people, splendidly engaged in church-planting throughout a small European country. The missionary who met me at the ferry warned me that 'tongues' is a dangerous topic in the churches and I should be careful about mentioning the Holy Spirit. The first girl who spoke to me in English said, 'You are a writer? Are you Pentecostalist or against Pentecost?' The pastor of the nearest church asked if he might have my advice about 'division over gifts'. The dormitory on a barge which I shared with young men that night had prominently on its shelf a book entitled, *Wat is Spreken in Tongen?* I needed no mastery of the language to guess the meaning of that! It is a story repeated everywhere. The energy and thinking of eager Christians is channelled into divisive and controversial issues.

There are other examples of the same danger of turning anecdotes into rules. Paul saw remarkable miracles during his highly successful mission to Ephesus (Acts 19:11–12). This may well teach us the principle that the church today should be concerned about healing and wholeness. It would be folly, however, to insist that the only way to evangelize a modern city is to mount a 'healing campaign'. The evangelists met a poor crazy girl in Philippi employed as a soothsayer. They discerned that she was demon-possessed and acted accordingly (Acts 16:16–18). It would be highly dangerous to suppose that here is a pattern, and that we must always meet irrational behaviour or mental distress with an act of exorcism. On the other hand we would be rash indeed to suppose that demon-possession now never happens.

We could go on. Offer *Acts* as a book of non-stop wonders which create rules of action for today, and we shall plunge into the artificial creation of excitement and a never-ending appetite for the thrilling and the emotional.

A right approach
We have dealt enough with negatives. If we should treat *Acts neither* as a blue-print for a miracle-a-minute adventure *nor* as a book of only historical interest pushed on to a

high out-of-reach shelf of dispensational curiosity, how *should* we treat it?

It must be allowed to speak for itself, in context, content and overall message. It is a book with a clear shape that teaches vital principles. Its anecdotes and adventures should be set within the explanatory context of the epistles which follow it but whose writing was contemporary with it. This can best be illustrated by an example which no one is likely to dispute.

In chapter 9 we have in vivid detail the story of Saul of Tarsus and his conversion from Phariseeism to Christianity. What shall we make of the details? How many of them constitute vital requirements for conversion? Saul was thrown to the ground by a physical or near-physical encounter with Jesus. Is that an essential part of conversion? He heard a voice speaking to him. Is that essential? For three days he laboured in lonely distress. A church leader gave him the laying-on of hands. He was filled with the Holy Spirit. He believed and was baptized. He promptly began to bear public witness to his faith. He did so by preaching. He seems to have won every argument in which he engaged. He travelled to Jerusalem and met the leaders of the mother-church. Now how many of these details are part of the essentials of conversion? Three days of distress? The laying-on of hands? The fullness of the Holy Spirit? Public witness? The ability to preach and argue? An encounter with the leaders in Jerusalem, or its equivalent? To find out, we discover what the rest of the New Testament teaches about conversion.

We will find that a genuine turning from sin is one essential, the new birth by the work of the Holy Spirit is another, a more-or-less public confession of Christ is a third (John 3:3; Romans 10:9; 2 Timothy 2:19). We are likely to arrive at the conclusion that baptism accompanies faith but does not automatically bring salvation (Romans 6:1–4). We will notice the pretty sharp remarks which Paul makes about freeing our faith from the domination of a priestly or apostolic hierarchy, real or imagined, in Jerusalem or anywhere else (Galatians 1:11–24). We will discover a variety of meanings for the laying-on of hands which do not link it essentially or exclusively with salvation (Acts 13:1–3; 2 Timothy 1:6–7). We will find that some Christians, but not all, are called to be preachers (Romans 10:14–15).

The exercise has been interesting and instructive. We are interpreting Bible narrative in the light of Bible teaching. It is an essential exercise in the art of hermeneutics. An anecdote standing on its own needs interpretation. What is its real significance? Which elements are essential and which incidental? What is God saying through it? Sometimes it will be self-interpreting (like, for example, the feeding of the five thousand coupled with Christ's comments drawn from it. John 6:1–14,32–40). More often it will require the comparing of Scripture with Scripture, the understanding of the incident from the doctrine. For the doctrine (if we are serious about Bible inspiration) is *God's commentary on the incident.*

This is what we must do as we reverently handle the *Acts of the Apostles.* Some of its incidents are self-explanatory or have the interpretation built into the narrative. As we shall see, the exciting events of the Day of Pentecost have explanation in advance (the promises of John the Baptist and Jesus) and explanation following (the sermon of Peter). As a matter of simple fact, neither of those explanations carries the thrust of a second experience after conversion infallibly demonstrated by the gift of tongues.

Luke–Acts: Jesus at work in the world and the church

We have to retrace our steps and look at the one Gospel which we have not yet examined. The connection between Luke and Acts is obvious, intentional and deliberate.[8] We can read them as one continuous narrative to which we can give the rather clumsy title Luke-Acts. Herein lies its great value. Part one (if we can so call it) describes the birth of Jesus, his mighty works and marvellous words, his death and resurrection. Part two describes the founding of the church, its works and its words, its adventures and its suffering, its calling of men and women to a fellowship of faith and love that realizes the presence of that resurrected Christ.

What links the two halves? Exactly what our consideration of John 14 and 16 has led us to expect. The ascension of Christ and the subsequent sending of his Spirit at Pentecost.

The very first words of part two sum it up powerfully. 'In the first book I have dealt with all that Jesus began to do and to teach' (Acts 1:1). *Began* – By implication, we shall now see what Jesus *continued* to do and to teach. But the first thing he does is to leave his disciples and return to heaven! That is no problem. It is an essential prerequisite to the world-wide continuation of all that Jesus began. Remember the promise in the upper room? '...greater works than these will he do, because I go to the Father' (John 14:12). Ascension ends the works of the localized Christ and releases the works of the spiritually-present Christ in every place. For ascension is followed by Pentecost. 'If I do not go away, the Counselor will not come to you; but if I go, I will send him to you' (John 16:7).

This is exactly what Luke-Acts now goes on to describe. The risen Christ commissions his disciples to be witnesses to the whole world, and promises the gift and power of the Holy Spirit (Acts 1:6–9). After his ascension the promise is fulfilled, and the church's great march forward begins with three thousand added that day and 'many wonders and signs were done through the apostles' (Acts 2:1-4, 37-43).

Key: the work of the Holy Spirit

This must not lead us to assume that the Holy Spirit is a newcomer to the scene on the Day of Pentecost. Part one is full of his activity in the life and ministry of Jesus. It is one of the unique contributions of Luke's Gospel.

The sacred mystery of the incarnation and virgin birth finds its focus in this. The mysterious and awesome promise is made to young Mary.

> 'The Holy Spirit will come upon you,
> and the power of the Most High will overshadow you;
> therefore the child to be born will be called holy,
> the Son of God.' (Luke 1:35)

The birth of John the Baptist has already been promised, [9] and he 'will be filled with the Holy Spirit, even from his mother's womb' (Luke 1:15). The two expectant women meet each other and celebrate with joy in an outburst of Spirit- filled prophecy (Luke 1:39–55). So does John's father a little later (Luke 1:67–68). The Spirit of prophecy has returned to God's people. There is an obvious link with the closing picture of the Old Testament. There Malachi describes the faithful remnant of believers who, in the day of apostasy, formalism and declension, meet often together and encourage one another to await expectantly the fulfilment of God's promises on 'the day when I act' (Malachi 3:16–17).

Their successors are now seen clustered around Luke's beautiful Christmas story. Simeon, a priest serving in the temple, awaits the fulfilment, the Holy Spirit upon him, and the revelation in his heart that he will not die until he has seen it. The same Spirit seals the promise within him, leads him to the temple just as the infant Jesus is carried in, and inspires another outburst of prophetic song (Luke 2:25–32). A prophetess Anna has very much the same experience, and shares its glad meaning with 'all who were looking for the redemption of Jerusalem' (Luke 2:36–38); successors to Malachi's believing minority.

Years later, Christ's public ministry begins, preceded by his kinsman John promising the baptizer in the Holy Spirit (the reference which Luke will pick up again at the ascension) (Luke 3:1–17; Acts 1:4–5). The ministry begins with Jesus' own baptism when 'the Holy Spirit descended upon him in bodily form, as a dove' (Luke 3:21–22).

Conflict immediately follows. 'Full of the Spirit' and 'led by the Spirit' Jesus endures a special time of temptation when the whole issue of that unique Sonship declared in his baptism is explored, challenged and settled (Luke 4:1–13). It is an inner battle immediately followed by external conflict, as 'Jesus returned in the power of the Spirit into Galilee' (Luke 4:14). With spreading fame following his words and deeds, he revisits his home town of Galilee and intervenes in the synagogue service. The Scripture he appeals to with stunning implication is the Messianic picture from Isaiah of one who can declare that the Spirit of the Lord is upon him (Luke 4:16–21).

The meaning of all this is clear.

In terms of Old Testament promise and purpose, the pieces of the divine jig-saw come together. Jesus accepts the double mission of Suffering Servant and Kingly Son. There is one Messiah, not two as some Jews speculated (puzzled by such different strands). He does so in the anointing and empowering of the Spirit of the Lord, that pinnacle-promise of Old Testament prophecy. Luke's Christmas narratives have prepared the way for it with their emphasis on the Spirit's mysterious work and the return of prophecy. The desert temptation and Galilee ministry follow logically from it. Since Satan is the 'god of this world' (2 Corinthians 4:4) his kingdom is threatened. Counter-attacks are foiled, suffering and sin are forced to yield ground, 'The Spirit of the Lord is upon me' (Luke 4:18) claims Jesus, and 'the power of the Lord was with him' (Luke 5:17) recall the onlookers. So self-evident is the work of the Spirit in Jesus' ministry that determined opposition to Jesus becomes, by definition, blasphemy against the Holy Spirit (Luke 12:10).

As the struggle reaches its dramatic conclusion in the apparent defeat of the cross, but the glorious victory of the resurrection, Jesus instructs his disciples in the expectation of the Spirit. As divine Son he is unique, but they as his followers may know the reality of the same Spirit. The Spirit-anointed will become the Spirit-Baptizer (Luke 3:16). The Father will 'give the Holy Spirit to those who ask him' (Luke 11:11–13). Faced with persecution, arrest, the pressures of a legal system turned against them, 'the Holy Spirit will teach you in that very hour what you ought to say', (Luke 12:11–12) (A promise, incidentally, which has nothing to do with carelessness and indiscipline in the preparation of sermons, CU studies or Sunday-school classes, but much to do with the unexpected crisis which stretches the disciple beyond his own ability). Finally, after the climax of cross and empty tomb, the risen Christ commissions his followers to a world-wide mission of witness. To equip them for that, he need only say 'I send the promise of my Father upon you;' (Luke 24:46–49). By this time they knew what he meant.

Acts: the Spirit at large

It is precisely a continuation of this theme that Luke picks up in his second volume. We have a brief replay of the closing Gospel events. The promised gift of the Father is again specified – 'before many days you shall be baptized with the Holy Spirit' (Acts 1:4–5).'These two passages (Luke 24 and Acts 1) unite the Gospel and the Acts in their continuous record of Jesus' redemptive ministry through the Spirit, first as the suffering Servant and then as the ascended King.'[10]

Acts, then, is to be understood in this light. So is Pentecost. What happened that day cannot be confined to the sometimes exotic (and often perfectly genuine) experience of certain Christians who need and receive an extra touch of the Spirit for some personal situation or public service. It is the culmination of Old Testament promise to all God's people reaching its apex with Jeremiah, Ezekiel and Joel. This is that, as Peter says succinctly (Acts 2:16). The New Age of the Spirit, long-promised and co-terminous with the Coming of Messiah, has now fully dawned. Or (to express it the other way) the Christ, exalted and glorified, freed from limitations of body and space, is widely at work, performing through his church those 'greater works' which were promised – greater, as we have seen, in number, nature and world distribution.

The rest of *Acts* amply illustrates this. As the infant church develops its organization, outfaces its opposition and expands its borders, the immediate, subjective and often visible work of the Holy Spirit is always the key. He was, as Michael Green has finely said, 'the architect of their success'.[11] The facts are so obvious on the surface and so well-known that one scarcely needs to check the references.

He was the inspiration of their mission. These early Christians saw men and women as perishing without Christ. With no hesitation or embarrassment they pointed to Jesus as the only hope of life for this world and the next. 'Filled with the Holy Spirit', Peter pleaded with men to 'Repent, and be baptized... in the name of Jesus Christ', (Acts 2:4,14,38–41) and three thousand responded to his plea. Commanded to give up their evangelism, Peter and John point to the witness of the Holy Spirit as their divine authentication (Acts 5:27–32). Stephen engaged in such powerful apologetics in the Hellenistic synagogues that 'they could not withstand the wisdom and the Spirit with

147

which he spoke' (Acts 6:10). Philip, already chosen to be a 'deacon' because he was 'full of the Spirit' pioneered missionwork in a Samaritan city, attracting crowds by the proclamation of his message, 'the signs which he did', the exorcisms and the healings (Acts 6:3–5; 8:4–8)[12].

Peter, reluctantly explaining the gospel to the Caesarean military household, sees the Holy Spirit 'falling' on his hearers, and his critical colleagues are compelled to admit that God had given despised Gentiles the same gift of repentance and life (Acts 11:15–18). Whilst church leaders are engaged in prayer at Antioch, the Holy Spirit launches them into the serious establishing of the Gentile mission and the evangelizing of the Mediterranean cities (Acts 13:1–3). The staggering success of this first mission shifts the centre of gravity of the Christian movement, but almost all acknowledge that the Holy Spirit has pre-empted the whole discussion (Acts 15:6–11).

He was the source of their strategy. We read nothing of church-growth conferences, missionary conventions and cross-cultural seminars. Maybe they did have their first-century equivalents, but the broad picture we are given is that of the direct strategy of the Spirit. The early Christians seem to have been hard put to it to keep track of the Spirit's activities and to make a pattern out of his planning. Apostles hurry to confirm Philip's rather outrageous work in Samaria (Acts 8:14–17), accept with some difficulty that Saul the persecutor is becoming Paul the apostle (Acts 9:26–30), acknowledge that the Spirit must know what he is doing in converting Romans (Acts 11:15–18), and celebrate with joy (after some heated discussion) his bringing of Asians to repentance (Acts 15:1–3).

Paul and his companions set about the systematic evangelization of the towns of Cyprus and Roman Asia, following the obvious trade routes. But intervention by the Holy Spirit changes their whole course and drives them into Europe (*cf.*Acts 13:4–6 with Acts 16:6–10). Divine intervention brings a further drastic change in Paul's methods, when rapid journeys are replaced by long periods of evangelism in Corinth and Ephesus.[13]

His was the guiding hand in their decisions. Like Christians in every generation, the first believers had difficult decisions to make. The Jerusalem church faced a near-collapse of its social welfare work with some rather nasty racial overtones. The disciples were as perplexed as we would be when their leaders were harassed, threatened, imprisoned and in some cases executed. Complex theological problems arose from an evangelism which steadily diluted the Jewish constituency in the church. How were the problems met? There seems to have been little evidence of either the hierarchical government of some modern churches or the democracy beloved by others. In ways not clearly specified, they reached their decisions. The process involved elements of argument, discussion, Bible-study, prayer, the exercise of prophecy, the opinion of respected leaders, and the sharing of spiritual experience. But three things are clear. They looked for the Spirit to guide them, they appointed Spirit-filled people to carry out their decisions (however humble the task) and they saw the result as joint-decisions of themselves and the Holy Spirit. With what must be either breath-taking arrogance or sublime conviction, they said, 'It has seemed good to the Holy Spirit and to us…'(Acts 15:28).

His was the source of their power. Remarkable energy was released by this emerging movement. Huge crowds were drawn to hear its preachers (Acts 2:5–6), a lame man leaped and walked at the command of its spokesmen (Acts 3:1–10), hypocrisy literally could not breathe in its atmosphere (Acts 5:1–6), prison gates swung open to release its captives (Acts 5:17–21), communities were stirred by its itin-

149

erant evangelists (Acts 8:4–8), remarkable miracles were performed by its messengers (Acts 14:3). In every case the energy was attributed to the Holy Spirit. But not all of his activities were declared in the obviously supernatural or in the apparent suspension of natural laws. In Paul's evangelistic journeys, physical miracle and moral change are equally, 'all that God had done' (Acts 14:27). Spirit-filled men are required to look after the Jerusalem soup-kitchen and pacify quarrelling widows from different racial backgrounds (Acts 6:1–6). The quality of fellowship, mutual commitment and financial sharing is seen as a striking work of the Spirit. In one breath, Luke describes as activities of the outpoured Spirit, 'wonders and signs done through the apostles', 'breaking bread in their homes' and 'glad and generous hearts' (Acts 2:43–47).

The model – Jesus. There is something even more impressive, and it clinches Luke's argument. Like a golden thread running throughout the picture of the early church is the reminder of Jesus. There are constant resemblances to his work, words and character. Like Jesus, the apostles heal the sick and announce glad news to ordinary people. Like him, they fall foul of the professional religious authorities and bear a calm witness on trial. The priests point out the resemblance in their own words. 'They wondered; and they recognized that they had been with Jesus' (Acts 4:13). In the story of Stephen the first martyr, the likeness is detailed and obviously deliberate (Acts chapters 6 and 7).

Stephen is a humble server, like the Master who came not to be served but to serve. Full of faith and power, he performs great wonders reminiscent of his Master's Galilee ministry. He bears noble and dignified defence as Jesus did before Pilate. He is cast out of the city and stoned, as the Saviour was crucified outside the city wall. He prays for the forgiveness of his murderers in almost identical terms to Christ's words from the cross. In the moment of dying he commits his spirit to Jesus, as Jesus committed his to the Father. Here is a man 'filled with the Holy Spirit' to such an extent that he reminds people of Jesus. What Jesus 'began to do and teach' is continued in his Spirit-filled followers and his Spirit-directed church.

The church – then and now

It is within this framework that we must view and evaluate the miraculous in the life of the early church. That in turn will help us to evaluate the supernatural in today's church – its absence or presence, its importance, its nature, its purpose.

We have seen that the 'natural' and 'supernatural' cannot be separated. Wholesale rejection of the miraculous on an *a priori* assumption that miracles do not happen leads us nowhere. Chapter 3 has illustrated that such an assumption is a non-starter. It can sound very scientific, but it is logical nonsense. Science assumes predictability and uniformity. It becomes impossible to speak in these terms without referring to 'laws'. Laws require a law-giver. By definition, the law-giver must be greater than the laws, and must stand outside of them. Therefore he can manipulate them and rearrange them in different combinations. That is no more immoral or absurd or logically impossible than it is for a man (who to some extent 'stands outside' because of his reasoning power) to manipulate the law of gravity and several laws of aerodynamics to make a jumbo-jet fly. There is no need at all to explain away the account of the early church in terms of superstition, exaggeration and myth, when it bears all the evidence of being an eye-witness account. Its claim to be a part of the inspired Word of God makes such an approach abhorrent to the reverent Christian anyway.

Nor should we go to elaborate lengths to disconnect the

151

Acts from the rest of the New Testament and deny its normative value. Of course Luke describes a special time; the blast-off to get the church in orbit, so to speak. Of course the period was unusual and unique in that the New Testament was not complete and in circulation. Of course (as we shall see in a moment) the apostles were a very special group of men in an unrepeatable situation. But when all that is said, the records remain. *Acts* describes the beginning of a new era, and in that era we still live. It could with equal accuracy be called the Day of Grace, the Age of the Holy Spirit, or the Church Age. In each case, we must admit that we still live at such a time.

The Holy Spirit came in a new way – and he came to stay. This is the long-awaited day in which the promises of Jeremiah, Ezekiel and Joel are fulfilled, and the Spirit of God works freely, broadly and distinctively. He comes not on occasion to prophet or priest, but 'upon all flesh' (Acts 2:14–21). That is one feature (verse 17). The other is the universal offer of salvation in Christ (verse 21). These are 'the last days' (verse 17) for God is making his last offer and performing his final work before the judgment and the end of all things. The writer to the Hebrews says the same when he reminds us that God who previously spoke by the prophets 'in these last days he has spoken to us by a Son' (Hebrews 1:1–2). It is his last word, and he has been saying it now for almost two thousand years.

We simply assert the same thing in different words when we call this the Church Age. We may differ semantically as to whether or not we can speak of 'the church' in Old Testament times. But certainly the complete thing is found for the first time in the New Testament. The secret purpose of God is now revealed, in the calling out of a people for God drawn from all languages, tribes and nations, inside and outside of the old covenant, a demonstration to angels, men and demons – foretaste, first instalment and promise of the day when all things will be brought into a unity in Christ (Ephesians 1:9–10).

This is how the first missionaries argued, in their preaching and their writing. Significantly, they reintroduced the well-used phrase 'signs and wonders'.

Peter's Pentecost sermon takes his hearers' minds back to 'Jesus of Nazareth, a man attested to you by God with mighty works and wonders and signs which God did through him in your midst' (Acts 2:22). The believing community which came to life that day saw 'many wonders and signs were done through the apostles' (Acts 2:43).

Some time later, threatened by the authorities, they pray for boldness to speak and for the stretched-out hand of God to heal and give signs and wonders (Acts 4:30). Philip the Evangelist spreads the news of Christ to Samaria, where an influential magician-priest is amazed by the 'signs and great miracles performed' (exorcism, and the healing of the lame and paralysed are specifically mentioned. Acts 8:7–8, 13). In Roman Asia, Paul and Barnabas remain in Iconium 'for a long time, speaking boldly for the Lord, who bore witness to the word of his grace, granting signs and wonders to be done by their hands' (Acts 14:3). A remarkable outbreak of the miraculous is seen in Ephesus, capital of the whole area; 'extraordinary miracles by the hands of Paul' in which even pieces of material which had touched his body were instrumental in healing and exorcism (Acts 19:11–12).

The purpose for us today.

What was the purpose of all this? When the message of free salvation in Christ was being questioned by legalistic Jewish believers, Paul and Barnabas related to the Jerusalem church 'what signs and wonders God had done through them among the Gentiles'. The context seems to imply that miracles of healing, gifts of the Spirit, the conversion of Gentiles and the subsequent moral change in their own lives all constitute these wonders (Acts 15:12).

153

At the same time, and to prove the same point, Paul was posing the question to those very troubled converts, 'Does he who supplies the Spirit to you and works miracles among you do so by works of the law, or by the hearing of faith?' (Galatians 3:1–5). The argument supports the evangelistic ministry of Paul, the truth of his message and the priority of faith in the Christian experience. Paul is more specifically defending his personal integrity and apostleship when he writes to the troublesome Corinthians, 'I was not at all inferior to these superlative apostles, even though I am nothing. The signs of a true apostle were performed among you in all patience, with signs and wonders and mighty works' (2 Corinthians 12:11–12).

The writer to the Hebrews sees the resemblance between Christ's ministry and that of the early church as a solemn confirmation that the same Saviour is at work in both. The seriousness of rejecting, neglecting or drifting away from such salvation is all the greater. 'It was declared at first by the Lord, and it was attested to us by those who heard him, while God also bore witness by signs and wonders and various miracles and by gifts of the Holy Spirit distributed according to his own will' (Hebrews 2:1–4).

Here then is the New Testament picture of the church, moving forward and outward, in the glorious conviction that Christ has conquered and now lives in them and works through them by his Spirit. There are strong resemblances between the remembered ministry of Christ and the present ministry of the church. The same gospel is proclaimed. The same forgiveness is offered. The same life-changing encounter is shared. In both cases the emphasis is much more on spiritual enlightenment and moral change than on physical miracles. The greatest wonder is not healed bodies or cast-out spirits, but new birth and the transforming process which follows, as 'we all with unveiled face, beholding the glory of the Lord, are being changed into his likeness from one degree of glory to another' (2 Corinthians 3:18). But words and works go together, moral change and mighty deeds mutually confirm one another. The church's message, like its Master's, comes to people 'not only in word, but also in power and in the Holy Spirit and with full conviction' (1 Thessalonians 1:5).

In the well-judged words of a contemporary theologian,

> Jesus' ministry has often been expounded in terms of the truth he taught and the compassion he showed. But inextricably bound up with these is the specifically charismatic dimension. He taught and he loved, with power and with authority to change people and things, and to do for them, and make happen in them, what his word declared and his love desired.[14]

The church is called to a like experience and a similar combination of word and works, of faith and power, of proclamation and demonstration.

That is the message, surely, of Luke-Acts. There may well be qualifications to that statement. We still have to look carefully at the uniqueness of the apostles and the completeness of the Bible revelation. We must always remember that both apostolic signs and (more generally) spiritual gifts are distributed 'as he wills' (1 Corinthians 12:11). We must not reduce the gracious working of the Spirit of God to a kind of magic which produces wonders-to-order designed to boost our self-esteem, confirm our spiritual progress or prove our denominational position. We should not develop a pathological craving for the spectacular. It is no sign of spiritual maturity to be forever rushing after the latest miracles because the everyday business of living in God's world is too humdrum. There is something unhealthy about a faith which needs constant doses of melodrama to sustain it.

There is danger too. The apostles themselves constantly

warned that the apparently supernatural is not always spiritual and divine. There is such a thing as 'the activity of Satan.... with power and with pretended signs and wonders, and with all wicked deception' (2 Thessalonians 2:9–10). We are not to be overawed by everything hard to explain, as if it were automatically from God. '...test the spirits to see whether they are of God; for many false prophets have gone out into the world' (1 John 4:1). Nevertheless, when we have said all this and sounded all these warnings, the fact remains. The Christian church is a supernatural organism, unique in the world of mankind. It carries a supernatural life and proclaims a supernatural message. *Acts* tells us so, and illustrates the fact with a practicality which we must not evade. In his church, by his Spirit, through his people, Jesus continues 'to do and to teach'.

Notes for chapter seven

[1]Eusebius, *Dem. Ev.* 3:4

[2]Justin Martyr, *Dialogue*, pp.254, 258, 308..

[3]Eusebius, *Contra Her.* II 61 & 62. Warfield points this out but is unsure of the significance.

[4]Justin, 2 *Apol.* 6 and *Adv. Haer.* 2:32. Fuller references are given in Michael Green's classic, *Evangelism in the Early Church* (Hodder, 1970).

[5]Augustine – for full quotations see Warfield, *Counterfeit Miracles* (Banner of Truth, 1972), chapter 2.

[6]Augustine – *On the True Religion* (390AD) & *On the Usefulness of Believing* (392AD)

[7]Augustine – *Retractions* (*see* Warfield, chapter 2)

[8]Compare, for example, the two prologues, both addressed to Theophilus, and the second avowedly continuing the same narrative as the first: Luke 1:1-4; Acts 1:1-5.

[9]Of course there is a difference. John's conception is very surprising and unlikely, but 'natural', and the infant then filled with the Holy Spirit. Jesus, is conceived within Mary by the overshadowing of the Holy Spirit.

[10]Charles Hummel, *Fire in the Fireplace* (Mowbray, 1970). I am indebted to this author for his whole analysis of Luke and Acts.

[11]See the argument of chapter 6 in Michael Green, *Evangelism: Now and Then* (IVP, 1979).

[12]It is almost universally assumed that the Philip of Acts is not the Philip who was one of the twelve in the gospel narratives, but 'Philip the Evangelist.'

[13]Acts 18:1-11 and Acts 19:1-8. In contrast to earlier brief visits to cities, Paul spends eighteen months in Corinth and well over two years in Ephesus.

[14]T. Smail, *Reflected Glory* (Hodder, 1975).

8

Great expectations

It is time to sum up, draw some conclusions, and underline a few lessons. To do so, I begin with a parable. Like some Bible parables, it is also a true story. If it is rather long, I can plead that it covers a rather long period of time; fourteen hundred years more or less. If it contains unlikely elements, I can at least vouch for a few of them. Accepted European history vouches for many more. Even the *British Medical Journal* adds its modest contribution.

A parable

In the mid-1960s, I was pastor of a church in the north-east of England, and chaplain of the local polytechnic. The church was in a tough working-class area of river-side Sunderland, once nicknamed the Barbary Coast because of its reputation. The congregation was evenly spread between working-class people, professionals, and college students who regarded it as the 'CU Church'. There was a love for truth, much life, a Bible-based ministry, and quite frequent overcrowding problems in the modest-sized building. Folk of all ages became committed Christians, and we had spells quite often when a conversion every week was normal.

The period was one of siege mentality and near despair in the churches generally. A panic plea for secular Christianity (*sic*) to meet man's coming-of-age, (*sic*) had led to a further abandonment of almost everything distinctively Christian, biblical and supernatural in the life and words of many churches. I personally knew one colleague who abandoned the ministry for social work because (he said) anything we can do, the State can do better. Two others were promoted from churches where their ministry to modern man had singularly failed to gain the attention of any modern men and emptied the pews. With a logic which evades me, one was promoted to principal of a theological college and the other gave his time to writing books telling the modern church how to do it.

Meanwhile, modern man had done another about-face and plunged out of the secular into the search for experience. Black magic, spiritualism, transcendental meditation, eastern religion, pyschedelic drugs, ouija-boards, horoscopes, automatic writing, mind-expansion; these became, not merely the activities of the way-out radical, but virtually of Mr and Mrs Average.

Nobody planned or advocated a change of policy, but our church found itself in new situations. Fresh converts or potential converts brought alarming problems with them. There were obsessive mental states, compulsive habits, and addictions, obscene depravities, frightening experiences, physical and emotional illnesses, and what looked like satanic activity.

The Word of God patiently preached, expounded, illustrated and enforced; that continued to be our principal tool. The gospel was offered with feeling and conviction to promote new life and a relationship with God. Prayer was encouraged and promises claimed. Some remarkable things happened. I have written about a few of them elsewhere.[1] I don't recall that any of us caught up in the events ever used the word 'miracle'. But we most certainly saw a few people healed of serious physical disorders, others rescued from acute emotional illness, others redeemed from addictions and others delivered from the kind of demonic power described in Bible accounts and modern missionary narratives. Several doctors in general practice, a specialist, and a psychiatrist were sufficiently impressed as to bring a direct Christian ministry of intervention into their professional lives.

Naturally, we gave the whole thing much thought. We studied the Scriptures and submitted experience to theology. We learned principles which all of us have quietly practised ever since, without making a great deal of fuss or uttering grandiose claims. Ironically, I found a reasonable amount of help in other writings of that very Benjamin Warfield whose strictures against any search for modern miracles I was well aware. He it was who reminded me powerfully of what I had long known.

The faith of the Bible is about a supernatural Person (God) who speaks in a supernatural revelation (the Bible) of the supernatural coming (by the virgin birth) of the supernatural Saviour (Jesus Christ) who in a supreme supernatural event (the resurrection) demonstrates that he has wrought a supernatural salvation (at the cross) which is focused in a supernatural experience common to every Christian (the new birth). Against such a background I found it unconvincing to argue that the Christian must not, however, look for supernatural interventions from God.

There were some other interesting features about Sunderland. Just down the road was the Church of All Saints where English Pentecostalism was born sixty years earlier. I knew about Pentecostalists. Warm-hearted evangelicals and unashamed Bible literalists, they also had less endearing characteristics. Like an unbalanced emphasis on wonderful doings and an irritating insistence that speaking in tongues is the sure and demanded sign of top-line Christianity. I did not agree with that then, and I do not now. But in other ways they provided a biblical rationale for much of what we saw happening. The Holy Spirit still supplies

159

to the church those gifts, rich in diversity, which it needed in the first generation to perform its tasks and still needs now. It was a proposition which I found irresistible in terms of Bible teaching and real experience.

Faith at an early age

Something else interested me more, perhaps because I love history and read it through slightly romantic spectacles. Nearer even than All Saints was St Peter's. Here, in the seventh and eighth centuries, the pious, gentle and scholarly Bede spent a lifetime. Moving between St Peter's Monkwearmouth and nearby St Paul's at Jarrow, the Venerable Bede exerted an amazing influence throughout Christian and pagan Europe. He was at the heart of a great flowering of piety, scholarship, civilization and spiritual growth. Rightly recognized as the first English historian (secular or sacred) Bede first introduced the serious study of history based on oral tradition, documentary evidence, eye-witness accounts, careful dating and the sifting of fact from fiction. This was second only in importance to his careful, laboured and loving translation of the Bible (he died whilst completing the last words of John's Gospel).

Now in his most famous work, *The Ecclesiastical History of the English People*,[2] Bede meticulously gathered and recorded the story of the second conversion of England to Christianity. Roman-Celtic Christianity had been pushed back into Wales and Cornwall as the legions left and the Saxons invaded. Bede wrote after the remarkable sequel, when through the labours of Celtic and Irish missionary-monks and the supplementary work of Latin missions, Saxon England became the nearest thing to a truly Christian country before the seventeenth century. Patrick and Aidan, Paulinus and Cuthbert, Iona and Lindisfarne, Morpeth and Jarrow; these were the people and places whose names rang like great bells in a story that has all the marks of the truly heroic.

Bede worked away at his desks in Sunderland and Jarrow to record a great story. And there the problem arises. It is widely acknowledged. Scholars write learned and slightly bewildered comments on it in their Introductions to every new edition of Bede. The story is shot full of the miraculous. There are remarkable happenings on every · page.

A church worker at Hexham slips on ice and fractures his arm, but is immediately healed in answer to prayer. A nobleman's wife at Barking 'afflicted by gradual loss of sight until she became totally blind' becomes possessed by a 'firm belief that she would be healed'. Helped to the church, she kneels in prayer, and walks home unaided and with perfect sight. John of Beverley exercises an unusually widespread ministry of healing which affects, among others, a dumb man, a girl with a horribly poisoned arm, and a thane's servant 'at death's door'. The stories are told with a wealth of circumstantial detail, often quoting eyewitnesses.

It is all very confusing. One modern ecclesiastical scholar has complained with some irritation that England seems to have been converted by a series of conjuring tricks. His bias shows. Many of them bear no resemblance at all to silly magic but are interwoven with high moral themes like penitence, prayer, humility, faith and submissiveness.

What are we to make of them? It is possible, of course, to dismiss them as the superstitious writings of a credulous age. There was certainly a unique off-beat 'otherness' about much Celtic thinking. Undoubtedly the Saxons were soaked in unpleasant superstition. Without doubt it all happened in an age when scientific cause-and-effect was unknown. And of course some of the phrases used are delightfully vague and non-technical by modern medical standards. But then so are many New Testament references. 'Sick of the palsy' (some kind of paralysis?). 'Full of leprosy' (some disfiguring skin-disease, but what?). 'Blind' (for what reason? cataracts? optic nerve destroyed?). 'Lame' (why? deformity? injury? hysterical?). The question, 'What *exactly* happened?' is answered no more easily of Bible miracles than of Saxon miracles, except that since the Bible is the Word of God we know that we can trust it. Can we trust Bede – not because he is a Bible writer but because he is accurate?

Everything else about Bede leads us to say 'Yes'. It is, again, a little like Luke the historian, without the addition of divine inspiration. Like Luke, Bede gets so much *right*. Are we to imagine, then, a scrupulous scholar who blazes a trail for scientific historical research, who pioneers education and culture, who alone provides us with the foundations of English history, who gets his lists of kings and abbots and grants and battles right, but who mixes the whole thing up inextricably with miracle-stories that are invention, superstition or credulous confusion? If he is right about the agents and the consequences but wrong about the circumstances, then what circumstances produced the consequences?

There is something else. Bede is writing about the two centuries before his own. In other writings he records contemporary and immediately-past events *and they are far less miraculous*. He does not claim that Northumberland lives in constant signs and wonders. He says that they happened in the great days of the Conversion. He muses on why they do not happen 'now'. His reasoning goes like this. They happened in the *Acts of the Apostles* because it was a time of divine initiative and planting; they were needed to get things going. So with the early days of Christianity in England. 'The Church was nourished with miracles in order that she might grow firm in the faith. When we plant bushes, we water them until they stand firm, but once they have taken root, the watering ceases'.[3]

Cuthbert, restless traveller between Melrose, Ripon,

Lindisfarne and the Farne Islands, was something of an exception amongst the late-comers in that he saw a good deal of the miraculous. But again there was a special reason. He was in effect, apostle to Northumbria. Plague often struck in those days and its horrors brought the strong temptation to apostasy, abandonment of faith, and revival of pagan magic. Even then, with moving simplicity, Bede records that the most frequent 'outward signs and wonders' of Cuthbert's ministry (the phrase is his) were that he 'delivered the poor and needy from those who despoiled them, took care to comfort the sad and faint-hearted, brought those who delighted in evil to godly sorrow, fed the hungry, and maintained frugality amidst the pomp of the world'.[4] A series of conjuring tricks? No – rather lives of godliness and spiritual power, spilling over into wonders from time to time.

A modern medical perspective

This is proving a long story indeed. Back in 1967 Sunderland, I delighted in the resemblances between Bede's records to (on the one hand) New Testament stories and (on the other) some of the things happening around me. A sharper mind than mine was observing it too. And in December 1983, a remarkable article appeared in that prestigious paper, the *British Medical Journal*. Chairman of the Sunderland branch of the B.M.A., Rex Gardner was the writer; one of those who had shared the Sunderland adventures.

The article bore a title which must be fairly unusual in that sober magazine. 'Miracles of Healing in Anglo-Celtic Northumbria as Recorded by the Venerable Bede and his Contemporaries: a reappraisal in the light of twentieth century experience'.[5] Mr Gardner gives a sympathetic nod to the difficulties modern scholars have with this ancient scholar in a day when 'scholarship' and 'belief in miracles' are mutually exclusive terms. But the question has to be answered. Were these patients healed as described or not?

He lists some cases carefully described in non-technical but vivid terms by Bede. They include broken bones immediately healed after a workman's fall whilst building the Hexham church, a Christian worker at Melrose collapsing in terrible pain but restored by anointing with oil, a woman at Jarrow healed of hideous ulcers after two successive acts of prayer, and a boy on the borders of Scotland raised to life after dying. He allows the obvious comment likely to be made, that none of the incidents is accompanied by anything like a modern medical diagnosis. But he then does something very remarkable.

He lists four parallel cases in recent times which were accompanied by careful medical diagnosis. A Lutheran nun in Darmstadt, Germany, was healed immediately of a broken leg sustained whilst building the community-church (and against the protests of the hospital doctor). A missionary in Nepal suffering agonies from a ruptured spleen was restored after anointing with oil. The ulcers story is matched by a Girls' Brigade captain in Monkwearmouth itself, healed to the astonishment of watching doctors after *two* times of prayer as in Bede's story.[6] The 'raising from death' story is paralleled by an Overseas Missionary Fellowship worker in Thailand – the parallel being detailed and including a power-confrontation, the jeers of pagan religious leaders, and the flight in panic of the opposers. Mr Gardner then goes on to give detailed clinical information about these and other remarkable healings which he witnessed in 'Bede country' in the 1970s.

He makes a powerful point. Had these details not been available (if we were looking at them over the centuries from the early days of the church or from the seventh century) we would have dismissed the stories as nontechnical, unproven, or open to other explanations. In fact it is of the nature of miracles to be open to other explanations, as we have seen. There is always an element of choice; always an alternative. We may believe or disbelieve. The very moment a miracle has become a past event, it is open to different conclusions. But *with the full facts available* the medical specialist makes out a very powerful case for the miraculous occasionally happening today.

Here ends the true story which is a parable. For it contains most of the elements which cause so much confusion, discussion and divided opinion when the miraculous is examined. What exactly defines an event as a miracle? The impossibility of other explanations? The elements of prayer and faith? The impressiveness of the result? The moral and spiritual change that it effects? Its obvious source in God's initiative? Its correspondence with biblical incidents? Its association with the truth of God? Its demand for faith? Its fortifying of faith?

The Christian today faces three kinds of problem as he looks at the subject. One is philosophical and emotional. One is theological. One is to do with practical misuse and misunderstanding, as he looks out over a very confusing scene in today's church.

A Christian world-view

We are all affected by the world-view in which we grow up, the presuppositions which are almost unspoken because they are taken for granted, the undefined but pervasive 'climate of opinion' which surrounds us. For the Christian in the Western world (especially Europe and Britain) that is *totally secular*.

'Secularisation', says Os Guinness, 'is the acid rain of spirit, the atmospheric cancer of the mind and imagination. Vented into the air by…computer terminals, marketing techniques and management insights, it is washed down in the rain, shower by shower, the deadliest destroyer of religious life the world has ever seen… Nothing is left to human spontaneity or divine intervention.'[7] The emptying of all spiritual and spontaneous factors out of life achieves the remarkable double effect of persuading man that he is virtually God, and at the same time of robbing him of his humanity. He becomes a cog in a vast impersonal machine. He becomes a collection of organic interchangeable spare parts in a body that has no meaning beyond survival. He becomes a number in a computer print-out. He finds himself as a meaningless speck in a self-perpetuating, self-explanatory mechanistic universe.

The Christian, by being born again of the Spirit of God, has been rescued from that machinery. He has been found by God and enabled to make the vital choice between two opposing philosophies which really have no further options between atheism on the one hand and belief in the personal, sovereign supernatural God of the Bible on the other. But he does not immediately and fully escape from the pervasive soul-destroying mind-belittling smog which surrounds him.

He can find himself a little bit embarrassed by the supernatural. Could not some sort of accommodation be reached? As he learns to 'think Christianly' (perhaps with the help of writers like C.S. Lewis, Harry Blamires, Francis Schaeffer) he will learn to shake off the feeling. Most of all, as he immerses his mind in the Scriptures and chooses ever more frequently and firmly to walk with God whatever the godless think of him, then the supernatural influence of the Spirit of God (usually quiet and undramatic, but sometimes intervening in more dramatic ways) will gradually enable him to speak with the apostle and say,

> Now we have received not the spirit of the world, but the Spirit which is from God, that we might understand the gifts bestowed on us by God (1 Corinthians 2:12).

So much for the philosophical-emotional problem. It

has to be tackled and overcome by an unashamed super-naturalism. What of the theological problem? This is of an entirely different kind, and comes from a totally different source.

Signs of an apostle

This probably represents the main thrust of reformed and evangelical thinking from the European Reformation until today. It must be taken seriously, for it raises fundamental issues of Bible authority and the submission we owe to Scripture.

Walter Chantry, one of its most eloquent exponents in print today, puts it as bluntly as this (he is writing of the supernatural particularly as it is sought among Pentecostalist Christians).

> Let there be no mistaking the central thrust of the charismatic renewal. It is offering the Church a new approach to authority and absolute truth…it is a *de facto* denial of the sufficiency of Scripture.[8] (My italics)

How can such a drastic charge be supported? The reasoning goes something like this. In the Old Testament, miracles are always connected with the revelation of God. Hence Benjamin Warfield's well-known phrase, *'Miracles do not appear vagrantly'* (*see* page 55). In fact, it could be reasoned, every miracle-working individual in the Old Testament was in the broadest sense a *prophet*. What happens when we open the New Testament? First comes the ministry of Jesus, and it is precisely a prophetic or revelatory purpose that his miracles fulfil. ('If I am not doing the works of my Father, then do not believe me' John 10:37.) Then there follows the ministry of the apostles, in which miracles are once more the authentication of the message ('The signs of a true apostle were performed among you'

2 Corinthians 12:12. 'It was declared at first by the Lord, and it was attested to us by those who heard him, while God also bore witness by signs and wonders and various miracles' Hebrews 2:3–4.)

The apostles of course had a unique role as original companions of Jesus, as witnesses of his resurrection, and as inspired writers of the New Testament (Acts 1:21–22; John 14:25). So again the purpose of miracles seems to be revelatory. The Old Testament prophet has become the New Testament apostle.

Now, goes the reasoning, *this purpose has been completely fulfilled*. Apostles and prophets were the foundation of the church (Ephesians 2:19–22; 4:11), and no-one goes on laying foundations for the same building; that job is finished. So the question *'Are miracles to be expected today?'* must be reframed as, *'Are apostles and prophets to be found today?'* and that in turn can be reframed as, *'Are men revealing the directly-delivered truth of God today?'* To such a question, no evangelical can give anything but a negative reply. The Bible is complete. There is nothing else to be revealed. Scripture is full of warnings (and church history is full of dire examples) of what happens when pretended revelations are added to the Word of God.

The Westminster Confession of Faith succinctly expresses what evangelicals have always believed.

> The whole counsel of God, concerning all things necessary for his own glory, man's salvation, faith, and life, is …set down in Scripture…; unto which nothing at any time is to be added, whether by new revelations of the Spirit, or traditions of men.[9]

This position, it has often been argued, renders impossible and wrong-headed the search for prophets, for apostles, for 'spiritual gifts' and for miracles. Such a quest becomes a rejection of the completeness of Scripture. So, says

Chantry, 'Pentecostal practice is a *de facto* denial of the sufficiency of Scripture. Neo-pentecostalists are seeking an additional word from God, a further source of truth. For them the Bible is not enough.'[10]

Protestant rejection of miracles

There is no doubt that this reasoning, if not quite this conclusion, represents the main thread of Protestant thinking. In Warfield's classic (written before the modern Pentecostal movement had begun) he argues, 'The Apostolic Church was characteristically a miracle-working church (but)…these gifts were not the possession of the primitive Christian as such…they were distinctively the authentication of the Apostles….Their function thus confined them to distinctively the Apostolic Church, and they necessarily passed away with it'.[11] Warfield does not in fact argue the case in detail from Scripture, but simply assumes it because it would be familiar to all 'reformed' churches anyway. What he does is to argue with great force that, this being the case, any hankering after miracles or charismata will inevitably go hand-in-hand with a departure from the authority of the Bible.

With a wealth of material he traces the growing worldliness of the established church after Constantine and the plunge into compromise, semi-paganism and superstition which produced the medieval Roman Catholic Church. It is almost embarrassing to read; embarrassing because it is true. Every species of absurdity, paganism, credulity, magic and crude wonder-mongering gradually found its place among the so-called miracles of the Middle Ages. Most of them were directly connected with practices at best highly dubious with no biblical warrant, and at worst in outright defiance of the clear commands of Scripture. The use of relics and indulgences, the worship of Mary, the promotion of 'saints' who were slightly cleaned-up and Christianized local deities, the working-up of superstitious emotion and hysteria; that was the seed-bed of the medieval miracle crop.

And this is the point; it was all practised by a religious establishment with two theological characteristics – the promotion of an exclusive priesthood in pretended succession to the apostles, and the wholesale abandonment of Scripture. The case seems proved. Miracles are for apostles. Apostles produced the Bible and came to an end. Seek more miracles and you are diverting your attention from God's truth which should be sufficient in itself. You may even find false prophets who will tempt you away from the Bible. Or alternatively, turn from the Bible to false apostles and they will supply you with false miracles, a product of human activity or even Satanic enterprise.

So Warfield reaches his conclusion. 'Pretensions by any class of men to be in the possession and use of miraculous powers as a permanent endowment are, within the limits of the Christian church, a speciality of Roman Catholicism. *Denial of these pretensions is part of the protest by virtue of which we bear the name of Protestants.*'[12]

Do the facts support this?

The argument is a disturbing one. It certainly ought to disturb any lover of the Bible and of evangelical faith. But is it in fact a fair argument, supported by facts?

Some of the events since Warfield's day may seem to say so. The non-catholic areas of the Christian scene have produced some very unpleasant examples of wonder-working movements which have the same two characteristics. They throw up powerful leaders who in fact go far further than the apostles ever went in demanding total and unthinking submission. They add further 'revelations' to the Scripture and gradually wean their followers away from the Bible altogether. The world of 'the Cults' is a weird and wonderful one; a sinister phenomenon which, however exotically varied within itself, displays common traits that are fraught with peril and are in total contradiction to the Word of God.

We must come closer than the Cults, too. There are movements which began among genuine evangelicals and which have taken on board theological error and moral disorder before our very eyes. They display the same marks. A cult of leadership supported by the 'wonders' of apparent miracles and deep internal commitment and community life, lead eventually to bare-faced and unashamed rejection of Bible doctrine and morality.

Other movements have not gone so far yet, but the spirit groans when one hears of leaders claiming to speak 'from the Throne', of services where semi-ecstatic 'prophetic utterance' is common but the Bible increasingly neglected, of enthusiasts who can point out on a map where God is present and which churches he has allegedly abandoned. There is great peril, too, in the oft-repeated contrast between 'experience' and 'doctrine' (to the detriment of doctrine). If purely subjective experiences are given priority over objective revealed truth, then the path can lead anywhere. Signs and miracles are not self-authenticating, but stand or fall in connection with the truth they profess to confirm.

Nevertheless, there are other facts of a happier kind too. The twentieth century has seen events which can be neither dismissed as recrudescent mediævalism nor condemned as cult-heresy. The *Pentecostal movement* worldwide has an honourable name for evangelism and biblical church-planting. It is the principal representative of the evangelical faith in vast areas of South America. It bears a noble record of defence of Bible authority and inerrancy, in contrast to shameful abandonment by more sophisticated main-line churches and theologians. Its unapologetic supernaturalism has set it four-square on the foundation of an inspired Bible and a heaven-sent gospel.

The more recent *Charismatic Renewal* (not an organized

171

movement but a tendency and an emphasis now affecting 20 million people) has remained evangelical on the whole, and has in several cases brought liberal or Roman Catholic people into a more biblical experience and faith. With very few exceptions it must be said that its emphasis on a miraculous ministry and even an avowedly apostolic ministry has *not* led to an abandonment of the Bible.

The new *house-churches* form a sub-division of Charismatic Renewal. Although some of their 'disciplinary and disciplining' structures give cause for concern, there is also an earnest determination to get to grips with great Bible issues which are of interest only to anyone who wholeheartedly accepts the authority of Scripture.

Another factor is not strictly Pentecostal or Charismatic in any directly derivative way. The phenomenal growth of *Christianity in the Third World* (especially Asia and Africa) does not spring from either of these two movements, but one of its main features is a strong sense of the supernatural and an experience of the miraculous. Careful church-growth studies reveal some interesting facts. Most Christians in the Third World have come to faith in Christ by mass movements quite unfamiliar to individualistic Western thinking.

These 'people-movements' (to quote the useful jargon) spring from the fact that in such areas the communities are inextricably linked in a way unknown to us, by family ties, communal living, shared activity or tribal life. The result of the preaching of the gospel is often at first total resistance to it (perhaps for years), then secret individual interest and finally multi-individual, mutually interdependent conversions. So, for example, Donald McGavran quotes the incident of *eight thousand* Dani tribesmen in West New Guinea declaring for Christ and burning their fetishes in one day [13]. Both Indonesia and Northern Nigeria have seen Muslim villages mutually agreeing to turn to Christ and turning mosques into churches.

Here is the interesting fact. Very often, 'people-movements' are marked by what might be called *power confrontation*. There is an established religion, often animism, but sometimes a more sophisticated religion like Islam or Hinduism: it directly clashes with the new gospel, and the conflict is sometimes settled by a striking intervention or answer to prayer. Indonesia has provided examples which simply cannot be dismissed as exaggeration. I have carefully questioned missionaries from Thailand and from Sarawak about similar incidents. There can be no doubt about the reality of the contest, the remarkable outcome, and the sturdy faith of the converts who responded as a result.

Now such incidents bear close resemblance to features of the Exodus confrontation, the ministry of Elijah, and the apostolic work in Samaria, Cyprus and Ephesus (Exodus 5 – 15; 1 Kings 17 – 2 Kings 8; Acts 8;13;19). Does the resemblance help us to find a way to an acceptance and understanding of the miraculous? Can we heed the warnings of the Calvin-Warfield view without needing to reject miracles wholesale?

Apostles – now and then
Certainly the apostles were unique *in their role as witnesses to the resurrection and writers of the New Testament*. But was the purpose of *the miracles* to bear witness to that uniqueness? The Hebrews 2 reference can be read that way. The 2 Corinthians 12 reference is rather less certain. Paul is defending his *personal ministry*, rather than his role as an inspired writer. In fact the 'signs of a true apostle' are listed in chapters 10–12, not merely in the much-quoted verse. They include powerful preaching that breaks down mental strongholds (10:1–6); the privilege of *first bringing the gospel* to these people (10:13–18); faithfulness to *divine truth* (11:1–6); unwillingness to be a *financial burden* to his converts (11:7–11); the endurance of great *hardship and suffering* for

173

the gospel (11:22–33); a deeply personal *semi-ecstatic experience* which he does not describe (12:1–6); and the 'patience, with signs and wonders and mighty works' (curious combination) referred to in the quotation (12:11–13). None of these factors is *unique* to apostles.

It is not at all clear, then, that miracles were a unique confirmation of apostolic authority and inspiration. To the Galatians they were a confirmation, indeed, of the *truth of the gospel of grace* which Paul preached (Galatians 3:1–9). In Samaria they were not performed by apostles but by Philip the evangelist and deacon (Acts 8:4–13). The Samaritan incident, in fact, is more like the kind of power confrontation of modern Third World 'people-movements'. Significantly it led to the same kind of result; the waning of Simon the priest-magician's influence, and the turning of a whole community to Christ. Exactly the same can be said of Paul's mission in Ephesus; the cult of Artemis was threatened and great numbers embraced the gospel (Acts 19).

The 'Conversion of England' described by Bede is another such example. Here again, the same factors prevail. False religion is overthrown, close-knit communities hear the gospel for the first time, power confrontation takes place, and the combined 'signs' of truth, holy living and divine confirmation lead to the greatest miracle of conversion.

Perhaps the concept of 'apostleship' has a wider meaning than the unique witness and the inspired writer (indeed, how many even of the original apostles *were* inspired writers? And how many of the inspired writers were not in fact apostles?). There is some New Testament evidence for a wider apostleship. Barnabas is called an apostle (Acts 14:14) and sees signs and wonders. So are Silas and Timothy, Andronicus and Junias (Romans 16:7; 1Thessalonians 2:6). Emissaries from the Jewish legalistic party could persuasively claim to be apostles (2 Corinthians

11:13). If *apostolic labour* is seen to be essentially the opening up of new territory to the gospel and the planting of churches, then *apostolic signs* can be seen as the special provision of God for the first impact of the gospel, the 'witness' of Hebrews 2, and the 'watering till the bush stands firm' of Bede. Miracles are then seen as indeed unusual, special, and selective, but not confined to the apostolic age.

This in turn fits the situation as we see it today where apostolic evangelism brings the gospel to new areas of the world and repeats the situation of Roman Asia in the first century and pagan England in the sixth century. Europe a thousand years later saw something similar when, through movements like the Anabaptists, a 'charismatic' ministry was clearly present. It embarrassed the first Reformers who feared to let things slip out of control and found themselves fighting on two fronts.

After the Reformation, John Welch, successor to Scotland's John Knox, saw seemingly well-authenticated miracles, including a raising from the dead. George Wishart witnessed the dreaded plague lapping up to the walls of Dundee 'in the form of a great black cloud' and then stopping in response to his fervent prayers.

Britain and America in the eighteenth century present a similar situation. The great Evangelical Awakening in these countries was associated with names like John and Charles Wesley, George Whitefield, Howell Harris, Jonathan Edwards and William Tennant. The supernatural was plainly evident. Edwards represented the most cautious reaction to it. In his *Distinguishing Marks of the Spirit of God* (1741) he carefully discriminates between the outward signs of high emotion or unusual phenomena, and the more reliable inward signs of love for Christ and obedience to God's Word. John Wesley was more responsive. He found the 'French Prophets' (a charismatic group) fascinating though disappointing. He carefully recorded cases of demon possession, exorcism and healing. He believed that the day of miracles had ceased, not because of the passing of the apostles, but because of worldliness, compromise, respectability and coldness of heart creeping into the church as it became 'established' in the Roman Empire…and in eighteenth-century England.

At such times of church-planting and the opening of countries to the gospel, it has been quite common for both pre-Reformation Christians and impeccable Protestants to speak of certain men as 'apostles'. Patrick was the apostle of Ireland, Aidan the apostle of Northumberland, Thomas Heywood the puritan apostle to the English Midlands, David Brainerd apostle to the American Indians, William Carey apostle to India. The English Baptists at one time had their 'messengers' (simply an anglicization of 'apostles') who opened new areas to the gospel and established churches.

Similarly today, a number of movements, charismatic and otherwise, have revived the title of 'apostle'. And whilst some of them make claims that are highly dubious on biblical grounds, others seem to use the word in this popular and secondary sense, not claiming special revelation or immense authority, but simply exercising a pioneer ministry and a superintendency amongst their churches. Of course one cannot build a doctrine on the popular and non-technical use of a word, but its persistent use does perhaps raise doubts over the very technical and exclusive meaning of 'apostle' which we are considering. Are the 'signs of an apostle' in fact what we can hope and pray to see at times of evangelistic expansion, renewal and revival?[14]

When we turn from 'apostolic signs' to the slightly different topic of 'spiritual gifts' we find even more questions over their abandonment on grounds of Bible authority. It is very hard to cement the charismata of Corinth, Rome and Peter's readership, into an exclusively apostolic framework. Certainly there is no clear New Testament statement that the charismata were apostolic or intended as signs of apostleship, or even that they had much to do with communicating gospel and truth. They were working abilities widely distributed amongst the churches, and designed to equip Christians for their task. They were not *all* supernatural or obviously miraculous. The need for many of them is still quite apparent, and some of them have never been missing. An appendix to this book examines them a little more closely.

To sum up, then… The Reformers and their successors were wise to be suspicious of new revelations and right to insist that the apostles had brought inspired Scripture to a close. Their warnings are still valid. But the argument can be taken too far. Miracles, though certainly appearing only at intervals, are not exclusively to do with the revelation of new truth[15]. There is a lot to be said for special intervention from God in confirmation of the gospel when it breaks new ground and makes an impact on new peoples.

Some guiding principles

There is a third problem of a more practical kind. Anyone but the most blinkered enthusiast can see that in what indeed looks like an age of restored signs and wonders, there are many dubious things happening and many 'mixed blessings' as a result. What tests, then, should be imposed on what claims to be miraculous? What should our attitude be to the supernatural? What place should it have in the life and experience of the average Christian and the normal church? There are some basic principles to keep in mind.

The question of authority

It cannot be said too often – signs are not self-authenticating. The fact that *something happens* does not automatically prove its origins in God. There are false prophets to be ignored, lying wonders to beware of, impressive psychic happenings to be treated with caution. Both enthusiastic friends and hostile critics of all things 'charismatic' should remember this. The mere fact of an exciting event does not guarantee divinity. Prophecies must be tested by their hearers, using God-given minds and God-given Bibles. Physical healings must be judged by their tendency. Do they glorify God and engage submission to his will? Or do they encourage an expectancy of undisturbed comfort? Or do they boost the claims of a religious leader? Or do they promote teachings and practices contrary to the Bible?

Warfield was absolutely right when he remarked of the healings at Lourdes 'We are far more sure that they are not from God than we ever can be sure... of how precisely they are wrought... That God is one, and that He alone is to be served with religious veneration, is no doubt an old revelation. It is nevertheless a true revelation. And he who takes it as such can never believe that (divine) miracles are wrought at Lourdes'[16]. The same could be said of remarkable results obtained by some 'spiritual healers' who are simply presenting spiritism in an attractive guise and thereby expressly defying the prohibition of Scripture[17].

The question of sovereignty
God acts how and when and where he wishes. By his creative power he controls the universe. Normally that control is exercised through the observed 'natural laws'. Occasionally he acts differently. The second fact is strictly no more and no less a demonstration of his omnipotent control than the first. To us, it is more impressive; it carries something of the nature of a 'wonder'. As the Bible makes clear, 'nature' cannot be viewed as an independent entity standing outside of God, but must be seen as one area in which God's will is at work. Both areas (of 'natural' and 'supernatural') not only demonstrate God's omnipotence, but express God's omniscience. He acts in certain ways *as and when he chooses*.

So it is futile to build elaborate edifices of theory to explain why God chose to act in particular ways in the past, and then restrict the expectation and even the possibility to similar times. God's interventions in the plagues of Egypt, the conflict with Baalism, the Babylonian exile, the incarnation of the Son of God and the establishing of the church, certainly have some principles in common. But they are hardly uniform events. One would not have guessed each 'next one' from each 'last one', if I can put it like that. As James Packer beautifully puts it – 'It is just like God (the God who uses the weak to confound the mighty) to have raised up, not a new Calvin or John Owen or Abraham Kuyper, but a scratch movement, cheerfully improvising, which proclaims the divine personhood and power of Jesus Christ and the Holy Spirit'.[18] God acts in dramatic ways and in remarkable gifts, 'as he wills' (1 Corinthians 12:11), 'according to his own will' (Hebrews 2:4), and 'to whom he will' (John 5:21). It is a wise man who avoids constricting his expectation of God within narrower limits than the Bible clearly imposes.

> The Lord is undoubtedly present with his people to assist them in all ages (says John Calvin) and when necessary he heals their diseases as much as he did in ancient times,...yet not by the hands of the apostles.[19]

A comment often made on present charismatic phenomena is that the great awakenings or revivals of Puritan times in America, Britain and Europe, were seemingly not accompanied by this kind of miracle. That is interesting and suggestive, but does not really prove anything. God may still choose to work this way this time if it is consistent with his glory. The European Reformation did not really fit the 'revival' pattern, but nevertheless much in it was a work of God. Many elements of the Wesleyan and the Moravian revivals of the eighteenth century did not fit too well either. There are indeed elements of Puritan awakenings desperately needed today (such as the fear of God, the sense of sin and the pursuit of holiness) but one period must not become the pattern to which all other events must conform in every detail.

The question of faith

God requires *faith* as the correct response to his revelation of himself. One facet of that faith is, in the words of William Carey, the Baptist pioneer missionary, to 'expect great things from God and attempt great things for God'. Other facets of faith are of course submission to God's will, and determination to put one's trust in the Giver rather than the gifts, the Instigator rather than the instruments.

It may well be that in today's world we need to recover from the panic created by arrogant self-sufficient theories that deny God. We must return to a more robust faith in the God who can do anything and who has entrusted to us a gospel inescapably supernatural. The pathetic prayer in the Authorized Version 'Lord, I believe, help thou mine unbelief' (Mark 9:24) might well be on our lips more often.

The question of abuse

The misuse and misunderstanding of the 'miraculous' is sadly widespread. However, the answer to misuse is not disuse. Rather we must improve our understanding, our expectation and our practice. There are some common areas of misuse.

Credulity. Faith is not a matter of screwing ourselves up to believe what is patently absurd. It does not serve God's glory to credit him with actions which any objective observer can see through. That includes claimed 'healings' which are mere improvements, 'prophecies' which are merely pious expressions of hope, the use of physical objects which are simply talismans, and the quoting of scriptural 'proofs' which are manifestly out of context and inaccurate.

Wondermongering. I coin the word to describe an almost pathological need which some Christians have to be constantly made to gasp. It is close to the attitude of Galilean crowds which saddened Jesus. In an account which can come only from Jesus himself (since he was alone at the time) we read that he recognized and resisted as Satanic the temptation to use marvellous powers to avoid physical discomfort, and to dazzle and impress others (Matthew 4:1–11). The need to have faith boosted by constant evidence of remarkable guidance, unusual provision and dramatic interventions is not a healthy one. Faith is nurtured on the Word of God, where his promises are claimed, his ways are vindicated, his truths are taught and his ways explained within limits imposed by himself.

James Packer has warned of the tempting attractions of the 'super-supernatural'; the constant longing for the remarkable. 'Undervaluing of the natural, regular, and ordinary shows him to be romantically immature and weak in his grasp of the realities of creation and providence as basic to God's work of grace'[20]. The Christian is commanded to walk by faith in the naked word of God; if God says something, that is sufficient..... or it should be. The Christian who is far more enthusiastic about miracles than about prayer, far more excited about dramatic guidance than about reading the Bible, is a believer who is running a temperature; it may make him feel warm but it is not an indication of spiritual health.

Anti-intellectualism. Some Christians badly misunderstand what the Bible has to say about the ability and foolishness of human 'wisdom'. In early chapters of his first Corinthian letter, for example, it is typical Greek philosophy that Paul is condemning. It relies on human intellect, clever and convoluted arguments and wordy rhetoric. It sounds very impressive. It finds the simplicity of the gospel offensive and ridiculous. But it simply does not bring men to the saving knowledge of God (1 Corinthians 1:18 – 2:16). Examples of it can be found often enough today in our places of education and our corridors of political power. The outpourings of some writers and poets and musicians and entertainers bear the same mark.

Unfortunately some eager Christians misunderstand this fact as an invitation to the believer to abandon his mind, his intellect, his mental discipline, even his common sense. Dramatic interventions of God in answer to 'simple faith' take the place of hard thinking, disciplined planning, careful reading, even study of the Bible. It sounds impressively biblical if one fishes out the occasional story from Acts and makes it into a principle. In actual fact it is the negation of New Testament teaching, which puts in opposition to *the fallen mind,* not excitement and drama, but *the renewed mind.* Much enthusiastic modern Christianity is weak precisely where the New Testament is strong …*in doctrine.*

> Be transformed by the renewal of your mind [not the abandonment of it], that you may prove what is the will of God (Romans 12:2).
> You…have become obedient from the heart to the standard of teaching to which you were committed (Romans 6:17).
> Follow the pattern of the sound words which you have heard …guard the truth that has been entrusted to you by the Holy Spirit (2 Timothy 1:13–14).
> Therefore gird up your minds… (1 Peter 1:13).

There is no substitute for hard thinking in the battle for truth which is being waged today. The airy dismissal of 'doctrine' in favour of experience simply will not lead to the robust militant Christianity which is needed to 'fight the good fight of faith'.

Special revelations. 'Illuminism' is a centuries-old phrase to describe something which is not at all new. It exerts a fatal attraction to some minds in almost every century. It is the claim to direct personal revelations from God which transcend the 'ordinary' experiences of disciplined prayer and Bible-study, and sit loosely to church discipline and corporate life. The illuminist constantly finds that 'God tells him' to do things. Often they are very odd things indeed. The more bizarre the idea, the more assuredly it must be from God. The opposite also obtains. *Unless* he receives some special insight or prompting or sign, the illuminist will hesitate or refuse to do a thing *even though the Bible commands it.* Of course, he is assuming that the promptings or the coincidences come from the Holy Spirit. But the Holy Spirit never contradicts himself. Nor does he (often) go out of his way to confirm with special signs a command which he has given in the Scriptures in perfectly clear and straightforward words.

A young man who assured me that God had told him it was all right to marry a non-Christian was simply deceiving himself; God had already told him not to (2 Corinthians 6:14–16). A lady who assured me that she would put right a quarrel with a fellow Christian according to the words of Matthew 5:23–24 *when the Holy Spirit told her to,* was condemning herself to a long wait; the Holy Spirit had already told her to, in Matthew 5.

Illuminists are often very sincere, very dedicated, and possessed of a commitment to obey God that shames more cautious Christians. Nevertheless they are treading a dangerous path. Their ancestors have trodden it before, and always with disastrous results in the long run. Inner feelings and special promptings are by their very nature subjective. The Bible provides our objective guide. Of course a mark of being 'sons of God' is to be 'led by the Spirit of God' (Romans 8:14) but the context of that whole chapter makes it clear that the 'leading' is a whole-hearted direction of the will, not simply occasional 'guidance'.

Illuminists quickly produce a special vocabulary of their own, in which normal words or familiar biblical phrases are given a special meaning that make lucid discussion very difficult. 'Formalism', 'legalism', 'pharisaism', become words descriptive of order, discipline and leadership. The 'soul' and the 'mind' are apparently inferior to the 'spirit'. 'Putting out a fleece' (once done by Gideon in a particularly hesitant mood) is preferred to taking godly advice or waiting on God in prayer. Committing the Word of God to memory or following a course of daily readings becomes, by some astonishing reversal of words, 'carnal'. In spite of all his sincerity and apparent spirituality, the enthusiast for special revelation is putting experience in opposition to Scripture, and labelling experience, 'the Holy Spirit'. Sad experience shows that when people are convinced that they are directly acting on behalf of God, it is time for the rest to run for cover.

Manipulation. This can take a number of forms, but they all spring from confusing spiritual communion with magic. The magician seeks to tap and use spiritual forces, psychic forces, occult forces, or any kind of energy that is available. The purpose is essentially selfish. The forces (whatever they are) oblige him and serve his ends, whether in giving him influence over people, material prosperity, a good harvest, or 'healing'. Balaam in the Old Testament and Simon the Sorcerer in the New Testament provide solemn warnings (Numbers 22; Acts 8:1–24). The Holy Spirit, on the other hand, is not a force to be used, but a powerful, glorious, gracious divine Person. He commands our obedience and invites our co-operation. He certainly does not hurry to answer our whims. He may be 'grieved' and even 'quenched', but he is not an impersonal force. The person who tries to 'use' the Spirit to prove a point, to demonstrate a spiritual superiority or to influence others to support him and follow him, is skirting perilously close to the edge of magic. He may well go over the edge and make a terrible discovery. The essence of the Spirit's work is that he sets us free to co-operate with him. The essence of the occult is that it drives and possesses. In fact the exploiter finds himself exploited.

Over-reaction. With such dangers in evidence, it is not surprising if some Christians react in disgust or embarrassment and close their minds to the possibility of the supernatural altogether. The temptation to over-reaction must be resisted. C.S. Lewis warned us in his delightful allegory years ago that Satan hails the magician and the materialist with equal joy. Denial of the supernatural destroys Christian living as effectively as obsession with it. We have to do with a God who is, by definition, *supernature*. The basic Christian experience is that of supernatural birth. The incarnation of the Son of God, his life, death and resurrection are fundamental to our salvation, and they all transcend the rules of this created world. The daily life of the Christian is possible only because the ascended and victorious Lord has showered gifts upon his people to sustain and equip them. The whole Christian experience is one of spiritual conflict against superhuman foes, in which natural weapons are useless.

When the believer engages in prayer, he is not talking to himself nor is he employing some psychologically reassuring exercise; he is addressing Almighty God who undertakes to answer, sometimes in a manner beyond anything we can ask or think. The answer is not a tap to be turned on; that is the path of magic again. The answer comes from one who has knowledge and wisdom beyond our comprehension, who holds the universe in his omnipotent hand, and who interweaves the whole incredibly tangled maze of human behaviour to work his will without destroying the genuine freedom and spontaneity of the events which he oversees. It is as if, in some unimaginable manner, a writer could produce a novel of immense length with huge numbers of characters who actually live and move and choose, and yet the final chapter brings the book to the conclusion which the author plans, 'according to the purpose of his will' (Ephesians 1:5).

Prayer is not the exercise of changing the will of that being, but of adjusting oneself to his will. The consequence will sometimes be very surprising. God does not have to obtain anyone's permission before he acts, nor does he carry a rule-book to consult. What he does is always, by definition, right and wise and good and just. He is indeed the God of the impossible. He will not restrict his actions to our expectations, and he will challenge our faith to move mountains as his hand moves our faith. More often than not, however, his intervention will be quiet, undramatic, orderly and even predictable. After all, he has acted often enough before, and explained his actions in quite some detail, in a book we call the Bible.

He has explained his purpose, too, as far as we are concerned. It is a moral purpose. He has not called us to be wonder-workers but to be saints. That is in fact the greatest wonder. The life which the New Testament repeatedly describes is a moral life. It involves repentance and faith, the putting off of old habits and the putting on of new. Even a glance at the apostolic writings makes this clear. The men who wrote these things once walked with Jesus. They were quite clear about his ability to turn nature upside down, walk on water, feed thousands with a few bread rolls, tell a storm at sea to behave itself. They saw a supernatural glory shine from his countenance. They saw disease flee at his presence and death crumble before him. They insisted that it all really happened. 'We did not follow cleverly devised myths... we were eye-witnesses of his majesty' (2 Peter 1:16). Similar things happened to them. They looked for another staggering supernatural intervention in the future, too. 'The day of the Lord will come ... the heavens will pass away... and the earth... will be burned up' (2 Peter 3:10). Claims of a self-organized mechanistic world of nature in which 'all things have continued as they were from the beginning of creation' were dismissed as nonsense (2 Peter 3:3–6). What quality of life, then, should believers in such a Saviour display? 'What sort of person ought you to be *in lives of holiness and godliness!*' (3:11).

Life surrendered to the will of God, submitted to the Word of God, transformed by the Spirit of God; that is the daily miracle to which God calls us in his Word.

Notes for chapter eight

[1] D. Bridge & D. Phypers, *More Than Tongues Can Tell* (Hodder, 1982).

[2] Bede, *History of the English Church and People* (Translated by Leo Shirley-Price, Penguin Classics, 1955).

[3] Bede, 'Commentary of Mark' in J.F. Webb & D.H. Farmer, *Age of Bede* (Penguin Classic, 1983).

[4] Bede, *History* Chapter 26.

[5] *British Medical Journal,* December 1983, 287(6409).

[6] This incident was witnessed personally by the present author.

[7] Os Guinness, *The Gravedigger File* (Hodder, 1983) p.61.

[8] Walter Chantry, *Signs of the Apostles* (Banner of Truth, 1983), p.22.

[9] Chapter 1, Article VI.

[10] Chantry, *Signs of the Apostles,* p.27.

[11] Warfield, *Counterfeit Miracles,* pp.5–6.

[12] Warfield, p.127.

[13] Donald McGavran, *Understanding Church Growth* (Eerdmans, 1970), p.304.

[14] A course offered by the Fuller Theological Seminary, significantly entitled *Signs and Wonders,* apparently draws more applicants than any other. It carefully works out this argument from the New Testament and from church history.

[15] In fact the Elijah-Elisha period does not really fit that pattern. It is not easy to see what advance in revealed truth was given at that time, and how those miracles were related to 'revelation'. Rather it was a time of confrontation with error, of a kind frequently witnessed since biblical times.

[16] Warfield, p.123. The word 'divine' is mine, inserted in this brief quotation to give the fair sense of Warfield's much longer argument. He willingly conceded that remarkable things happened at Lourdes. His question was – do they come directly from the God of Truth?

[17] For example, in Deuteronomy 18:9–22 and Isaiah 8:19–22. In both of these Scriptures, God does not condemn occult practices simply because the pagans do

them, but expressly because by its nature, enquiry into the occult is a rejection of the divine revelation given and the divine limits imposed.

[18]James Packer, *Keep in Step with the Spirit* (IVP, 1984), p.230.

[19]Quoted by A.W. Pink in *Divine Healing – Is it Scriptural?* (Evangelical Press, 1977), p.25. Pink does not give his reference source.

[20]James Packer, *Keep in Step with the Spirit,* p.194.

Appendix 1_____

Miraculous healing in the church today

This is a subject which arouses strong feelings and is beset by competing claims. As often happens, both extremes tend to overstate their case. One of the most unfortunate results has been a tendency of Christian doctors to dismiss the subject out-of-hand and a tendency of Christian lay-people (medically speaking) to adopt an anti-medical anti-intellectualism which almost regards resort to a physician as an abandonment of faith.

Christian doctors tend to make the following points:

(a) Claims of healing have no value if there was no reliable diagnosis before the incident.

(b) The psychosomatic element enters very largely into many apparent healings. Everything from asthma to the ubiquitous 'back-trouble', from arthritic pain to apparent signs of cancer, can often have a hysterical or neurotic cause. If this cause is removed by the assurance of pardon, the resolving of fear or the ending of a relationship-problem, then physical healing may well result. Doctors are usually reluctant to regard that as a 'miracle' since it has a possible explanation in terms of human knowledge.

(c) Many Christian doctors insist that a truly miraculous cure should, in accordance with Bible incidents, be immediate, total, permanent, clearly organic, and inexplicable in terms of human knowledge. Many of them will maintain that they have never witnessed such a cure.

(d) Most Christian doctors have met patients whose hopes were falsely raised by some itinerant 'healer'. They were then left either in a state of pathetic self-deception (claiming a healing quite clearly not received) or in a state of cynicism or depression because nothing happened, or because they are accused of 'not having enough faith'.

With humility, and with great respect for the Christian medical profession, I would want to make the following replies:

(a) In the few cases I have seen of remarkable healing, I have worked carefully alongside of doctors who have given the diagnosis and confirmed the cure. I wish that were more often true of the claims sometimes made.

(b) Psychosomatic illness is immensely widespread and the cause of an ocean of sorrow, suffering and darkness. Its healing by the sharing of gospel implications seems to me to be something that glorifies God and is a sign of his Kingdom. Whether or not it is technically 'miraculous' is to me superfluous. This book has already argued that a strict division of 'natural and supernatural' along lines of 'explicable and inexplicable' is not altogether biblical.

(c) I am not at all sure that those conditions are fairly demanded, or are fulfilled in the Bible miracles. Do the stories of Elijah/Elisha and the gospel narratives give us clinical details which deny the possibility that some illnesses were psychosomatic? Are terms like 'leprosy', 'sick of the palsy', 'lame', *etc.* meant to represent scientific diagnosis in modern medical terms? In any case, Christian doctors can certainly be found who have witnessed cures which fulfil all of these requirements, and have been convinced. I know personally of a serious blood-disease over which the words 'inexplicable recovery' were written on the medical card, of a horrifying varicose ulcer which was healed in the presence of two doctors, and of a case of cancer in the shoulder and neck which, after prayer, was found on the operating-table to have disappeared. Is there not a danger that in insisting on the 'medically inexplicable', we are slipping back into a 'God of the gaps' mentality?

(d) The matter of unfulfilled hopes and exaggerated promises is desperately serious. Pastors probably meet as many sad examples of it as do doctors. It would be a blessing for everyone if there could be a moratorium on certain itinerant campaigns with the 'come-and-see-a-miracle' kind of publicity. The crude and simplistic equation of 'faith' with 'results' is harmful, misleading, and a caricature of real Bible teaching. The mockery of the high Christian virtue of submission to God's will which some 'healers' indulge in should be abandoned once and for all. It diminishes saints of God, almost infinitely superior in godly walk, to the level of those who make fun of it. It gets very close to denying the sovereignty of God which is his glory, and encourages the sought-for sovereignty of our wills which is our shame. Dubious equations of physical healing and the atonement should be avoided. The absurd assertion that recourse to a doctor is 'lack of faith' should be abandoned. It has no biblical support, is a form of mental blackmail, and is a statement unworthy to fall from Christian lips.

A positive approach to healing might include the following principles:

1. Sickness is related to sin and to the fall. That does not mean that an individual illness is related to an individual sin. But it does mean that in broad terms, sickness is an enemy and a work of the Enemy. The idea of 'wholeness', on the other hand, is closely related to biblical concepts of holiness and of salvation.

2. Holy living is likely to lead to healthy living. Other things being equal, the Christian who keeps God's laws is less likely to fall prey to certain physical illness (like cancer from cigarette smoking, ill consequences of overeating and overdrinking, venereal diseases, *etc.*) and may well be more immune to psychosomatic illness caused by stress,

worry, guilt, fear, loneliness, jealousy and anger.

3. The gospel carries with it implications for changed life-style, changed attitudes, community acceptance and refuge from guilt, which may in turn have further consequences in mental, physical and emotional healing.

4. The church is the natural place in which this healing influence will be at work. If it is conceded that 'gifts of healing' are available, then this is the place for their exercise – not necessarily in public on Sunday, but within the fellowship which is structured and led as it should be. Observation would suggest that a ministry of healing could have several possible expressions.

It may happen spontaneously through the *preaching and teaching of God's Word*. This, above all else, directs our gaze to the promises and purposes of God. It may happen equally spontaneously in a *sacramental context* of Communion or Baptism. This is not, of course, through veneration being given to the elements of water, bread, wine, *etc.*, but simply through Word-and-Sacrament together, drawing the attention of the believer to the glory of Christ, the completeness of his Word and the fullness of his promises. When I see this happen spontaneously indeed I rejoice and am not surprised. I would hesitate to encourage it deliberately, since the human heart so naturally turns to idolatry. If our fallen nature can possibly find a loop-hole for trusting in the symbol rather than the Reality, the creature rather than the Creator, the gift rather than the Giver, then it will gladly do so.

A more deliberate and organized ministry may be exercised through *counselling*. With open Bible and sympathetic hearing the pastor or leader shares in the problems and pains, the discoveries and the pitfalls, the joys and the sorrows of the growing Christian. Sometimes hurts from the past will be uncovered. Sometimes wrong relationships will be adjusted. Sometimes harmful attitudes will come under the correcting influence of Bible instruction, advice and prayer. In my last church we had a team of twelve trained people (three of them doctors) who worked in this way with the pastoral team and the eldership, to considerable effect. Both *anointing* with oil and the *laying-on of hands* have scriptural precedent. If seen as a focusing of faith, a sharing of fellowship or a symbol of openness to the will of God, their value is obvious.

5. Satanic attack is a biblical reality, and there can be no reason for doubting that it still happens today. The Enemy may use an already-present ailment (physical or nervous) to sap faith and cloud vision. Especially where there has been dabbling in forbidden areas of the occult and so-called spiritualism, there can be a more direct demonic influence to which the victory of Christ over the god of this world needs to be applied.

6. It is biblical to consider the possibility that some sickness may be the result of God disciplining the wayward child whom he loves. One would expect that removal of the disobedience would then lead to removal of the sickness.

7. Even if both apostolic gifts and more general charismatic gifts are abandoned as 'not for this age', we have the potentially awkward instruction of James 5:13–16 to cope with. As redoubtable a Puritan as Thomas Goodwin (1600-1680), though rejecting apostolic and charismatic gifts in the usual 'Reformed' manner, warned, 'In rejecting Holy Unction (the strange Catholic version of James 5 which turned it into the Last Rites) the Reformers went too far, even denying....that blessing which God in mercy hath appointed'. A.W. Pink, a 20th-century Calvinist similarly asks, 'If the healing cults have gone to one extreme of unbalanced fanaticism, have not most of the Lord's people gone to the opposite extreme – that of unbelieving stoicism or fatalistic inertia?'[1]

8. There can be no doubt that modern western Christians have become so accustomed to the 'scientific thinking'

which permeates our society, that we experience real difficulties in accepting emotionally the concept of God's direct intervention. Perhaps a clearer commitment to the biblical world-view will help here. It will involve (I have suggested) a glad acknowledgment of the sovereignty of God in all areas of life and activity. It will not try to maintain a strict dichotomy between 'natural and supernatural'. It will point the physician back to the old concept expressed in phrases like, 'I bind up the wounds: God heals'. It will help him to recognize God's goodness in some forms of 'alternative medicine' and in answered prayer.

9. Christian doctors, like all other Christians, must allow their faith to be challenged at times. A general practitioner writing in the journal of the Christian Medical Fellowship has suggested, 'Perhaps (we) subconsciously feel (miraculous healing) as a personal threat – a rather impudent invasion into our own painstakingly-learned and much-respected domain of expertise? Our patients are hardly likely to be impressed by arguments in support of biblical miracles of 2000 years ago, coming from those who patently never expect them to happen today.' He concludes, 'The large volume of recently-published accounts of a wide variety of miraculous healings must surely awake renewed interest....Let all of us see to it that we are not like the people of Christ's own town, of whom it is written, *"he did not do many mighty works there because of their unbelief"*.' (Matthew 13:58).[2]

Notes for appendix one

[1]Both quotations from A.W. Pink, *Divine Healing – Is It Scriptural?* (Evangelical Press, 1977).

[2]'Charismatic healing – some personal reflections' by Trevor G. Stammers, in *In the Service of Medicine*, vol. 29:4, no. 116, October 1983, pp. 18–22.

Appendix 2_____

Charismatic gifts

Thirty years ago there was almost nothing written on the 'charismata' outside of main-line Pentecostal circles. Nowadays, thanks to the Charismatic Movement, one can sometimes be pardoned for wondering whether anyone writes about anything else! The purpose of this appendix is simply to relate the New Testament charismata to the subject of this book which is both wider and more narrow.

1. *Charismatic gifts in the New Testament were working-abilities distributed to the churches*. They were provided to equip the church for its task. The need for many of them was obvious then, and is still obvious today. Some of them have never been absent from the historic church. 'Tongues' and the corresponding 'Interpretation' are probably the only ones likely to raise an eyebrow. I have never been convinced that these two have been totally absent for eighteen centuries. (D.L. Moody certainly experienced them at the Sunderland YMCA in 1873. They were known in France in the seventeenth century). On the other hand, rather vague and undocumented claims that they have always been around are equally unconvincing.

2. *On the New Testament evidence, many of the charismata were not miraculous or supernatural at all*. Some of them clearly were. Apparently 'natural' gifts were 'teachers … helpers, administrators' (1 Corinthians 12:28–31), and 'service … teaching … exhorting … liberal contributing …

giving aid... acts of mercy' (Romans 12:6–8). Obviously miraculous gifts (mentioned in these same references) included 'gifts of healing, working of miracles...the ability to distinguish between spirits'. Gifts difficult to define as either natural or supernatural, and related either to mental illumination or high emotion, were 'the utterance of wisdom, the utterance of knowledge...prophecy...various kinds of tongues, the interpretation of tongues'.

3. *The New Testament does not exclusively link charismata with the apostolic office.* We have seen that this link is often assumed, but it reads too much into the clear statements of the Bible. Gifts were evidently in wide use among the early Christians. The same applies to the oft-repeated assertion that charismata were invariably or principally associated with *revelation*. The Bible does not say so. The fact that the New Testament was not yet complete is never given as the reason for the charismata being granted. The idea that they were withdrawn *when* the New Testament was completed, finds no clear expression in its pages. The list of them that we have already examined gives little support to such an idea. Why should acts of mercy, generosity, teaching or praying in tongues, be necessary only until the Bible is complete?

4. *There is no New Testament basis for dividing sharply between the normal and less-normal gifts.* Calvinists tend to assert that the miraculous gifts were associated with apostles and the non-miraculous gifts are the 'normal' provision for everyday church life. Pentecostalists often argue that the miraculous gifts are limited to those who in every age are 'baptized in the Spirit' and the non-miraculous are more widely found among the uninitiated or unblessed. Neither assertion can be proved from Scripture, and the intermingling of both kinds of gifts in the same Corinthian chapter militates against both views.

5. In quite clear New Testament teaching, the gifts are associated, not with apostolic activity nor with a restricted

second-blessing, but with the doctrine and the metaphor of the church as the body of Christ. This is obvious in the passages quoted already. 'Just as the body is one and has many members ... so it is with Christ' (1 Corinthians 12:12. Then follows the long and careful argument against quarrelling, pride, jealousy or dismay over the varied expressions of spiritual gifts, for it is by this variety that individual Christians function as limbs – 'members' – in the body). 'For as in one body we have many members ... so we, though many, are one body in Christ...Having gifts that differ...let us use them' (Romans 12:4–6). The argument is the same as to the Corinthians, the word 'gifts' – *charismata* – is the same, and one member of the list is prophecy.

The reference in 1 Peter 4 does not specifically mention the body (it is characteristically Paul's metaphor) but again the word for *gift* is *charisma* (verse 10). This association of thought is vital, for it lifts the discussion of charismata above any divisive theories. All Christians are members of the body of Christ, whether they live in the apostolic age or not, whether they have had a pentecostal experience or not. Gifts bring variety-in-unity, not division; in the New Testament, anyway. If they bring something very different today, perhaps we should be looking rather hard at them, our Bibles, and ourselves!

6. *Spiritual gifts are not self-authenticating.* This fundamental principle is forgotten amazingly often by exponents and opponents of modern charismata alike. It is of the most important gift of prophecy (and the one which is most easily assumed to be direct-from-God and without-fear-of-contradiction) that Paul insists on the need for care in accepting or *rejecting.* 'Let two or three prophets speak, and *let the others weigh what is said*' (1 Corinthians 14:29). What purpose does the 'weighing' have? (AV and GNB – 'judge', NEB – 'exercise judgement', NIV – 'weigh carefully'). 'Do not quench the Spirit, do not despise proph-

esying, but test everything' (1 Thessalonians 5:19–20). Test it for what?

Numerous Scriptures give us the answer. Sadly, gifts may be exercised in an unruly manner, a divisive manner, a foolish manner, a self-glorifying manner, an unloving manner. That is the whole assumption behind Paul's teaching and warnings to the Corinthian Christians, especially in chapters 12 to 14. Prophecy itself may be false prophecy. So warns the apostle John. The spirit of Antichrist (religious error) is at work as well as the Spirit of Christ (who is the Truth). So – 'do not believe every spirit, but test the spirits to see whether they are of God' (1 John 4:1). Impressive exercise of gifts may not be accompanied, necessarily, even by true faith and Christian obedience. Jesus tells us so, specifying prophecy, exorcism and mighty works – performed by some to whom he will eventually say, 'I never knew you; depart from me' (Matthew 7:21–23).

A grasp of this fact again cuts both ways in the charismatic-anticharismatic argument. Whatever charismatic gifts *are,* they are *not* such overwhelming evidence of the direct and dominating work of the Holy Spirit that the human is swamped, the possibility of error removed, and infallibility guaranteed. A prophecy may be true or false. An inward impression may be helpful or misleading. A tongue may be language or nonsense. An interpretation may be accurate or mere wishful thinking. A remarkable healing may be an act of God, an emotional response, the result of strong suggestion, organic, psychosomatic, complete, incomplete, permanent, temporary, divine, human or demonic. The mere act itself, whether prophecy, tongue, healing, or whatever, is not the guarantee of divinity. We must not say, as some do – 'If it moves, it is God.' Nor must we say as others do – 'If it moves, stamp on it.'

But equally, if the mere exercise of a charisma is not automatically right, nor is the false exercise of a gift (or its intermingling with human frailty and error) sufficient reason for dismissing the whole subject as nonsense. We do not do that with other more familiar spiritual exercises. There have been some pretty shocking preachers, but we do not therefore dismiss preaching. Some private prayers are mere wishful thinking and some public prayers are mere disguised scolding or lecturing, but we do not therefore abolish prayer. Jesus warns us that some almsgiving has wrong motives, but we do not therefore deride Christian generosity.

By what standard do we test charismata? *There is the test of love.* Paul's thirteenth chapter to the Corinthians is not a parenthetic 'Ode to Love' but an integral part of his argument. Both of the other 'charismatic chapters' similarly link the exercise of love with the exercise of gifts (Romans 12:9–10; 1 Peter 4:8). Are gifts exercised in a manner that is 'patient and kind', or 'jealous, boastful, arrogant, rude'? Does the gifted Christian 'insist on his own way'? Does he 'rejoice' at the (to him) obvious failures of his less blessed brother and the evident shortcomings of his more traditional and cautious fellow Christian? (1 Corinthians 13:4–7). And of course the same questions must be pressed upon those who 'don't believe in the gifts' because (they feel) their theology is more balanced and their knowledge more profound. For neither tongues nor understanding nor knowledge, nor even what claims to be 'faith' are of any value at all if they are loveless (verses 1–3).

There is the test of experience. What in practice does the exercise of a particular charisma lead to? What is its tendency? When the impressive words and the thrilling feelings are stripped away, what in fact is left? If some reference to the future is involved, is it accurately fulfilled? If a healing is involved, does it last?

There is the test of purpose. In all of the relevant New Testament references, the purpose of the gifts is to build up the body of Christ, to strengthen the church, to benefit the believing community, to increase the happy and complementary integration of Christian people and their varied abilities. This is most eloquently summed up in the famous Ephesians 4 passage where the word charismata is not actually used, but where the risen and exalted Christ is portrayed as granting gifts (verses 7 & 11 from which we get *donations*) to his church. The reason is given; 'to the saints for the work of ministry, for building up the body of Christ' (verses 12 – 13). Paul has returned once more to the metaphor of the body. The purpose of the charismata is body-building.

There is the test of Scripture. A charisma always has an element of the *subjective* in it; sometimes a very strong element. It is *happening* to me (or him, or them). The Bible by way of contrast is *objective*. It stands there outside of us, untouched by our experience – confirming or casting doubt on our experience – totally divine – unmixed with human error and infirmity. To this touchstone we bring our experiences, our feelings, our impressions. The Bible confirms, explains, amends or even contradicts our experiences which we *hope* are experiences of God. The process is not reversible; at best our experiences can only highlight, underline, or bring into subjective enjoyment what the Bible says. Always the place of authority must be the Bible. Even in that most stunning of experiences, the series of appearances of the resurrected Christ, he drew their attention back to the Scriptures. 'Beginning with Moses and all the prophets, he interpreted to them in all the scriptures' (Luke 24:27), 'Then he opened their minds to understand the scriptures' (Luke 24:45).

Only by imposing on signs, experiences, visions and gifts *the authority and the judgment of Scripture* can we save ourselves from being lost and confused in a welter of happenings and startling events. Apart from that authority and judgment, we put ourselves in the same position as mediaeval mystics, superstitious sign-watchers, members of fanatical cults and victims of spiritualism and the occult. On the other hand, lack of faith, failure in expectancy, reservations about God's power and purpose, cold intellectualism and negative attitudes, will all conspire to prevent us from enjoying the wealthy variety of gifts offered by a gracious God who wills our good and has undertaken to equip his church adequately for her task and calling.

Appendix 3_____

Prophecy, revelation, authority and guidance

If prophecy is assumed to be directly inspired by God, authoritative and infallible, then clearly there can be no prophecy today. The Bible is complete. There are no more Isaiahs. There will be no more apocalypses after the book of Revelation. However, there is no need to force all prophecy into such a definition. The Bible contains all prophecy which God so overruled and providentially recorded that it became part of the canon of Scripture. There was plenty more which was never recorded in Old Testament times, and the office and activity of prophets (good, bad and indifferent) was a familiar ingredient of Israel's life. The promise was that when the Spirit of God was poured out, prophecy would be more widely known, and indeed practically universal, among God's people (Joel 2:28–29; Acts 2:14–24).

Acts describes a church scene in which prophets had their place, for example warning of the danger of a famine (Acts 11:27–28) or the peril faced by Paul in travelling to Jerusalem (Acts 21:10–11). In the Corinthian church (and by implication elsewhere) prophecy was to be regarded more highly than some other gifts because it promoted understanding and church-building (1 Corinthians 14:1–5).

Paul gives a kind of practical definition of prophecy (1 Corinthians 14:3). 'He who prophesies speaks to men for their upbuilding and encouragement and consolation.' (As is often said, prophecy is more concerned with forth-telling than foretelling). It did not carry some self-contained authority, but was to be listened to, sifted, and judged (verse 29). In Antioch the prophecy of coming famine led to a sensible voluntary social welfare scheme (Acts 11:27–30). Paul decided that Agabus' prophetic warning of peril in Jerusalem was not sufficient to stop him going there: the local Christians read it that way, but Paul presumably saw it simply as a call to courage and determination in spite of danger – or perhaps as a warning to the locals – 'Face up to it... you are not going to see him again, and he needs your prayers.' He prayerfully made up his own mind (Acts 21:12–14).

There seems no reason to believe that prophecy must always come in an oracular style, or that it will appear only in 'open' unstructured worship where everyone is free to take part audibly if they wish. That is certainly the format at Corinth, but the Corinthian way was clearly not the *only* way to do it. Nor is there any biblical reason to suppose that prophecy will always be prefaced by, 'Thus saith the Lord', or delivered in the first person singular as if God were directly addressing the listeners... ('I say unto you'...'O my people!'...'I will bless you'...*etc.*). Indeed, such a custom may serve only to confuse 'normal' prophecy with inspired canonical prophecy in the Bible, and discourage the hearers from that very 'weighing' exercise that God requires of them.

It should be a common experience for Christians gathered in numbers large or small to hear Bible teaching, sermons, exhortations, advice, which prove to be truly *prophetic*. Preaching and teaching should always be in a general sense *from God* for all present (because it is biblical). But often some part of it will prove to be *specially* from God, with a very *particular* application to one or more hearers. Someone feels 'this is for me', 'this is the very thing I was worried about', 'this is what I must do'. Preachers

203

should pray for this and expect it to happen frequently, perhaps always. Hearers should gather expectantly, listening for it, looking to God for it, and willing to respond to it.

What authority does prophecy carry? The same authority as that of any other Christian activity in the church, like leadership, counselling, teaching. If it is biblical, it will carry the certainty that the Scripture always brings to those who believe the Bible. If it is true, it will prove to be true. Spiritual people will respond warmly to it. Wise and proven leaders will approve and confirm it. The enlightened conscience will embrace it. Of course the response to it will be no more infallible than the prophecy itself. The prophet may be mistaken in thinking he speaks from God and the hearer may be mistaken too. But that is the risk we take with *every* Christian activity. It is exactly why we must 'test'. Infallibility is found only in the Bible – not even in our interpretation of that!

Is prophecy a provision for discerning God's will? Obviously it is *one* such provision. It does not carry some self-contained authority not possessed by other means of finding God's guidance, such as the studying of Bible principles, the emulating of Bible examples, seeking advice from mature Christians, following conscience, noticing the trend of providential circumstances in a world ruled by God, and employing one's reasoning powers renewed by the Holy Spirit and in submission to God's Will and Word.

Know the truth

BRUCE MILNE

'You will know the truth,' said Jesus, 'and the truth will set you free.'

Christians have already begun to know God and his truth. This handbook will help us to grow in that liberating knowledge, as it opens up the great themes of God's Word and shows us how they fit together.

Each chapter looks at one facet of biblical truth and encourages further study with Scripture references to look up, questions for discussion and books for additional reading. The main sections all close with practical reflection on how the Bible's teaching challenges us and moves us to adore the living God.

288 pages   Large paperback

Inter-Varsity Press

Keep in Step with the Spirit

J. I. PACKER

Understanding the Spirit is a crucial task for
Christian theology at all times; honouring the
Spirit is a crucial task in Christian discipleship
today.

Is the church in danger of overemphasizing or
quenching the Spirit?
What are today's acts of the Holy Spirit?
Is charismatic life something new or unique?
Are modern spiritual gifts the same as those of
the New Testament?

Dr Packer considers these questions in the light
of Scripture and Christian history, and issues a
radical challenge to personal and corporate
revival.

> '. . . this is a helpful, timely book which has
> much to teach the Church today.' *Christian
> Weekly Newspapers*

302 pages   Large paperback

Inter-Varsity Press